Initiative

A course for advanced learners

Student's Book

Richard Walton
& Mark Bartram

CAMBRIDGE
UNIVERSITY PRESS

PUBLISHED BY THE PRESS SYNDICATE OF THE UNIVERSITY OF CAMBRIDGE
The Pitt Building, Trumpington Street, Cambridge, United Kingdom

CAMBRIDGE UNIVERSITY PRESS
The Edinburgh Building, Cambridge CB2 2RU, UK http://www.cup.cam.ac.uk
40 West 20th Street, New York, NY 10011–4211, USA http://www.cup.org
10 Stamford Road, Oakleigh, Melbourne 3166, Australia
Ruiz de Alarcón 13, 28014 Madrid, Spain

First published 2000

Printed in the United Kingdom at the University Press, Cambridge

Typeface Joanna 12pt, Officina Sans 16pt *System* QuarkXPress 4.03

ISBN 0 521 57582 6 Student's Book
ISBN 0 521 57581 8 Teacher's Book
ISBN 0 521 57580 X Cassette

Contents

Map of the book

4

Grammar	Writing and discourse focus	Listening topics	Speaking and pronunciation	Learner training
Articles	Discourse markers Punctuation		Word stress	Storing vocabulary
Review of futures	Brainstorming for ideas	Food intolerance (Hearing perception)	Weak forms of auxiliary verbs	Storing vocabulary
Habits and characteristics	Formal letters	An unusual town (Hearing perception)	Elision Discussion: travel	Dictionary use
Reported speech and questions	Achieving formal style Correction	Ram-raid story	Sentence stress Discussion: police and the community	
Relative clauses		(Hearing perception)	Contrastive stress	
−ing forms	Giving examples	Financial facts and figures	Silent letters Discussion: money and morality	
Conditionals	Leaflets	Bush babies (Hearing perception)	Linking	
'Past' for distancing	Using examples to create coherence		Word-class pairs	
Any and some	Adding detail	Reflections on school		Keyword grid
Using participles	Choosing correct register	Telling a story (Hearing perception)		
Positions of adverbs	Problem-solution evaluation	Urban problems		Using a grammar book
Future forms	Revising and editing	Michelangelo (Hearing perception)	Unstressed endings	
Multi-word verbs	Improving your style	Gadgets (Hearing perception)	Nouns from multi-word verbs	Finding sources of real English
Noun combinations	Ordering an argument	Correcting two charts	Compound words	
Fronting for dramatic effect	Achieving dramatic effect	The News Quiz		Storing vocabulary

To the student

Welcome to *Initiative*. We hope you enjoy using the course, and that it enables you to progress in your English.

Initiative aims to

- teach you new language;

- consolidate the language you already know;

- encourage you to explore different ways of thinking about language learning;

- develop good study habits which can be used outside the English classroom.

About the course

The map of the book on pages 4-5 shows you how the course is organised and will help you to plan your studies and chart your progress.

The Starter Unit introduces you to good study and learning habits by making you think, talk and read about language learning. The activities here will help you throughout your studies.

There are 15 main units, each based around a theme which we hope you will find interesting and relevant. The main focus of these units is on the skills of reading and writing.

Listening activities are included, with a variety of recorded dialogues and interviews; these are signalled by the headphones icon.

Hearing Perception exercises aim to help you to understand authentic speech spoken naturally.

Grammar sections, on a blue tint, encourage you to 'rediscover' the rules of structure and usage for yourself. For a more comprehensive grammar reference book, you may like to refer to *Advanced Grammar in Use* by Martin Hewings (Cambridge University Press 1999) or *Practical English Usage* by Michael Swan (Oxford University Press 1995).

There are frequent vocabulary exercises and work on collocations, and you are encouraged to use a good monolingual dictionary, such as the *Cambridge International Dictionary of English* (Cambridge University Press 1995).

Each unit ends with a review section which refers back to the previous unit. This will help you revise and consolidate what you have learnt. Review exercises are indicated by the 'rewind' icon.

Tapescripts for all the recorded material can be found at the back of the book.

We wish you success with *Initiative*.

Richard Walton   Mark Bartram

Starter Unit

SU.1 Are you a good language learner?

a Do the following quiz. You may tick more than one answer to each question. Try to be as honest as you can! (See page 160 for the answers.)

Are you a **good** LANGUAGE LEARNER?

1 When you start a course in a foreign language, do you know what you want to get out of it?

a yes, always
b yes, sometimes
c no, never

2 Do you know more or less what level you are now?

a yes
b no

3 When you learn a new piece of language, do you try to practise it afterwards?

a never
b occasionally
c sometimes
d usually
e always

4 Do you try to understand the rules of the language you are learning?

a not really, I just try to speak it as well as I can
b yes, I think it's important to understand the rules
c I'd like to understand the rules, but sometimes there are so many exceptions that it's impossible!

5 How do you remember new vocabulary?

a I don't!
b I write alphabetical lists in my notebook
c I revise new words regularly
d I write lists with translations
e I draw pictures

6 Do you check your work before you give it to the teacher?

a always
b sometimes
c occasionally
d never

7 Do you ever have any contact with English speakers?

a no, I don't live in an English-speaking country, so it's difficult for me to meet them
b yes, I am living in an English-speaking country now, so I meet them every day
c yes, sometimes: I try to meet them as much as I can even though I don't live in an English-speaking country
d it's not important for me to meet English speakers, so I never do

8 What do you do when you feel depressed about your English?

a I think to myself: 'Everybody gets depressed about their English sometimes; I must just carry on ...'
b I go and do something else for a bit
c I take up aerobics instead
d I think about learning another language instead

9 How do you feel about learning English? (Be honest!)

a I hate it, but I have to do it!
b I like it most of the time, but sometimes it's rather dull and boring
c I love it
d I have no feelings about it – I just need to do it for my work or my studies

10 How do you feel about **either** British **or** American **or** Australian culture?

a I am not interested in it at all
b I am quite interested in it
c I am very interested in it
d I am not really interested in it, but I realise I need to understand it in order to understand the language better

b Now discuss your answers with your partner. Which answers would the 'perfect' language learner give?

c Read the following passage and decide what the 'right' answers to the quiz might be.

WHAT MAKES A GOOD LANGUAGE LEARNER?

We all know that some students are better at learning a foreign language than others. Why is this so? And what is it that makes for a good language learner? The writer H. H. Stern has identified four basic factors. ⁵

The first of these is the ability to develop an active learning strategy. In other words, good language learners have the ability to select goals and sub-goals, ¹⁰ and recognise the stages and sequences of their learning.

Secondly, they are able to see the language as a formal system with its own rules and relationships between forms ¹⁵ and meanings. Furthermore, they analyse the language and develop techniques of practice and memorisation. They can check their own performance, and revise it in order to progress. ²⁰

The third way is to develop a social strategy for learning. This means that good learners understand that, in the early stages, they will be vulnerable and dependent, and can accept this. However, ²⁵ they also seek contact with native-speakers of the language. They work out ways of dealing with difficulties in the language. And finally they become actively involved as participants in authentic language use. ³⁰

The final area is psychological or emotional. All language learners will have emotional and motivational problems while they are learning. In spite of this, a good learner will cope effectively, and ³⁵ will cultivate positive attitudes towards themselves, towards language learning in general, and the target language, society and culture.

SU.2 ## Setting goals for yourself

It is useful to set yourself some goals and sub-goals which are practical and achievable.

a Look at the following areas of language study and decide what your main goal is for each one.

Example: **reading**

I would like to be able to read magazine articles in English.

reading	writing	listening
speaking	grammar	vocabulary
pronunciation		

b Now find out from other students whether your goals are the same or different from theirs.

SU.3 ## Devising a programme of work

It is a good idea to develop a programme of work – when, and for how long, you are going to study English each week. But this programme will be different for every person – you have to develop your own personal programme of work.

a Answer the following questions.

1 How much time per day can you afford to spend on your English?

2 How will you divide this up? Will you use it all for grammar, for example?

3 At what time of day do you like studying best? Early in the morning? Late at night? (Don't say 'never'.)

4 Do you like studying in short bursts (say, 30 minutes at a time), with lots of short breaks, or do you prefer longer stretches (one to two hours)?

5 Is there a particular place that you find you can study better?

6 Do you like listening to music while you study or do you prefer silence? If you do like music, which kind?

b Veronica is studying English in her own country. She has made a weekly study programme. Look at her chart. Discuss it with your partner. What parts of it seem strange?

	Morning	Afternoon	Evening
MONDAY	Lessons	Study	Free
TUESDAY	Lessons	Study	Free
WEDNESDAY	Skiing	Skiing	Study
THURSDAY	Lessons	Study	Pub
FRIDAY	Lessons	Study	Study
SATURDAY	Intensive revision	Football	Free
SUNDAY	Church/Free	Study	Study

c Now write a weekly chart for yourself.

(SU.4) Recording and remembering vocabulary

a What does the following graph show? Discuss your ideas in pairs or groups.

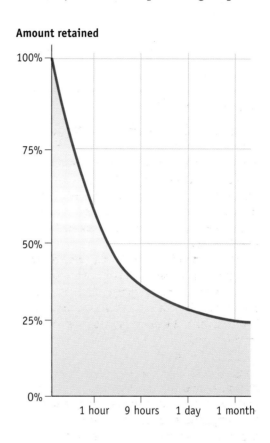

Amount retained

You probably said that it shows us how quickly we forget new vocabulary. So it is important to record vocabulary in an interesting and memorable way and devise ways of **recalling** it.

b Work in pairs and discuss the following questions with a partner:

1 What do you do with vocabulary that you have just learned?

2 What do you do **later** (the next day, the next week, the next month) to recall it?

c Many students simply record new vocabulary by writing it down, perhaps in alphabetical order, with a translation into their own language. Did you or your partner think of other ways of recording vocabulary? Here are two ideas for recording vocabulary that make it easier to recall it.

1 BRAIN MAP. This is a good visual way of storing and remembering words or phrases which relate to the same topic.

Write some more words and phrases in the bubbles on the right.

2 SYNONYMS AND ANTONYMS. Another good way of recording vocabulary is to put words that mean the same (synonyms) together and words that mean the opposite (antonyms) together. But be careful! Two words rarely mean **exactly** the same thing!

Here are some examples:

pound (£) = quid (informal)
huge = gigantic
blow up a tyre = inflate (formal)
hardly = barely (only just)

old-fashioned ≠ trendy
smooth ≠ rough
deep (water/thoughts) ≠ shallow
good at ≠ hopeless at

Organise these words into pairs of synonyms or antonyms in your own vocabulary notebook.

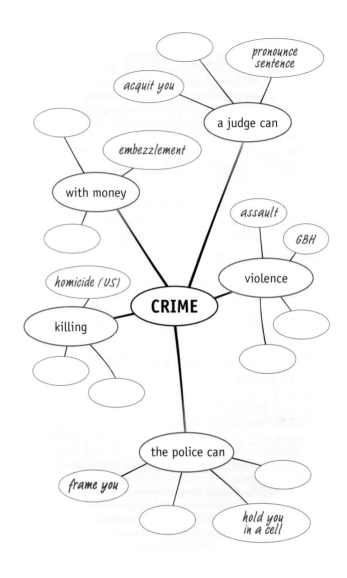

There are other ideas for recording vocabulary in Units 1, 2 and 15 of the book.

d Finally, you need to try to activate the new vocabulary you want to learn by:

● using it in the next class or homework;

● writing the word or expression in a sentence you invent for yourself;

● watching out for the new expressions in reading or listening activities;

● writing or telling a crazy story linking all the new words and phrases you want to learn.

Now you try writing a crazy story, using **eight** of the new words on this page. You are not allowed to write more than 100 words.

SU.5 The importance of collocation

A collocation is when two words (or sometimes more than two) are seen together frequently. In English, these are very common, and it is a sign of a good English speaker to be able to use collocations well. There are several exercises to do with collocations in this book.

a Decide whether the collocations (in **bold**) in the sentences below are possible or not. Use a good English-English dictionary if you have one.

1 Don't forget to **slide the curtains** before you go to bed.

2 The garden's **bone dry**. I hope it rains soon.

3 Sue's always **immaculately clothed** when she goes out.

4 It was a very deep cut and was **bleeding greatly**.

5 Keith usually goes for the **soft option**.

6 I **decided for** the yellow one in the end.

7 Patrick was **full asleep** by nine o'clock.

8 Mary could hear **thunder banging** in the distance.

9 They were all **delighted at** the news.

10 We had a long wait so we **burnt time** by playing cards.

b There are many types of collocations in English. In the box below, there is a list of nine types.

1 adjective + noun
2 verb + noun
3 noun + verb
4 verb + adverb
5 verb + preposition
6 noun + adjective
7 adjective + adjective
8 adverb + adjective
9 adjective + preposition

Look at the following collocations, and put each of them into one of the nine categories in the box. There are two collocations for each category.

1 interested in

adjective + preposition

2 breathe deeply

3 make a mistake

4 quietly confident

5 a spare tyre

6 wide awake

7 dogs bark

8 apologise for

9 rock hard

10 a narrow escape

11 deadly serious

12 hideously ugly

13 regret something bitterly

14 good at (maths)

15 tell the truth

16 dog tired

17 spend (money) on

18 school breaks up

c Use one of the above collocations in each of the following sentences. Sometimes you will need to change the form of the words in the collocation. The first one has been done for you as an example.

1 By the time we finished climbing the mountain, we were *dog tired* .

2 If you get very angry, the best thing to do is to .... for ten seconds.

3 If you drive a car in Britain, it is obligatory to carry .... with you.

4 On the night before his birthday, Jack was still .... at midnight!

5 On what date do the .... for the summer holidays?

6 A liar is a person who doesn't always ....

7   George had worked very hard all term, and when the exams came, he was feeling ....

8   The passengers had a .... when the two planes passed within a few metres of each other.

9   The person who never .... , never made anything.

10 When the boy told me to give him my wallet, I thought he was joking, but when I saw the expression on his face, I realised he was ....

SU.6 The importance of discourse

A text in English (or any language) is not just a series of unconnected sentences. If the text is well-written, the sentences and the paragraphs link well with each other to make it clearer.

a Work in pairs or small groups. Put the text in boxes 1–13 in order. Box 1 has the first sentence.

b Underline the words and phrases which helped you decide.

SU.7 Choosing a good monolingual dictionary

Dictionaries are a marvellous resource, but not all dictionaries are the same, and deciding which one you should buy is an important choice. Apart from meanings, what else should a good dictionary provide you with?

a In pairs, write a list. Think about the following areas:

collocations and idioms	grammar
pronunciation	spellings
multi-word (phrasal) verbs	style
word formation	punctuation

1 Have you ever wondered why some students do much better in exams than others?

2 And they schedule their time well – maybe aiming to finish homework a couple of days early.

3 No, what seems to count is the way you study, according to the experts: the pupils who get the best grades have a series of techniques to help them.

4 For example, they keep their rooms or studies in good order – so they don't waste time looking for pens or important papers.

5 Finally, they don't worry too much about what other people do, or what they think of them. If they feel happy studying in the bath, they study in the bath!

6 And these are the same whether you're studying in London or Los Angeles!

7 In that way, if it takes longer than they think, they'll still be in time.

8 To sum up, it doesn't seem to matter *when* or *how much* or *where* you study: the most important thing is how.

9 When they take notes, for instance, they mark the important points in red so when they're revising later, they can see the more relevant material immediately. But if they *don't* understand something, they will ask the teacher immediately.

10 Secondly, good students develop good studying strategies.

11 Hard work isn't the whole story either. Some of the best students actually work *less*.

12 Firstly, successful students tend to be tidy and well-organised.

13 Intelligence is not the only answer – the most academically gifted pupils do not necessarily perform best in exams.

b Look at the examples below and decide what type of information is being given in each case. Choose from the words in the box below.

example sentences	collocations
word formation	usage/style
cross-references	word stress
alternative spellings	pronunciation
varieties of English	
grammatical information	

1 / dʒi:nz /

2 / rɪ'tɜ:n / OR / rɪ't<u>ɜ:n</u> /

3 **wagon**; also **waggon**

4 n(C), n (U), (V), adv, adj (pred), pron (usu sing)

5 (fml), (infml), (derog), (GB), (US), (esp Scot), (sl), (lit), (taboo), (fig)

6 **box of tricks** → **TRICK** OR **bag of bones**: see **bone**

7 **boundless energy/enthusiasm** OR **bootleg liquor/cassettes**

8 **boss, bossy** (-**ier, iest**), **bossily, bossiness**

9 (**brainchild** / breɪntʃaɪld / n (sing) a person's own plan, invention or idea:) **The new arts centre is the brainchild of a wealthy local woman.**

10 **pavement Br** / peɪvmənt /, **Am side-walk**

13

Lost
for words

a Look at the following list of words. Try saying them to yourselves. Then divide them into words you like or dislike purely according to the sound.

petal	slime	wriggle	portly
sloth	miasma	terrapin	fang
conker	grubby	zigzag	yo-yo

b Compare notes with another student, and see if you agree or disagree.

c Now find out from a dictionary or from your teacher what the words mean. Do you still like or dislike them?

a Read the three texts below quickly. Do not spend more than two minutes on this. They are all on the topic of words. Which text talks about:

1 a new word?

2 words that children use?

3 word games?

The 'average' one-year-old uses two or three words with meaning but mostly she is still holding babbling conversations involving plenty of gestures; her high-chair is her soap-box. Her first words are what linguists call 'holophrases', 5 a single word being equivalent to a phrase or sentence. For example, 'mama', can be a command or a request; it can mean 'Mummy, I want that toy', or 'Hurry up with my dinner', or just 'Come here'. A word like 'dog' can be applied to any animal at 10 first; it may mean 'Look what the dog is doing', or it may be used to express any other thought about the dog.

In contrast, at this stage, a phrase such as 'all gone' is used like a single word. The baby hears speech 15 as blocks of sound, not as a series of words. She reproduces the parts of the block which she associates with certain things; if she always hears the words 'all gone' together, they equal one word to her and you cannot really claim she is yet joining 20 up words. True word-joining, such as 'Daddy come', begins around the age of eighteen months, although it may occur later (see Late Talker, p. 484).

Text 1

Text 2

One of the more lovable characteristics of human beings is their persistent tendency to find new and often frivolous uses for things. Words were designed for the serious business of communication but humans constantly devise novel uses for them. [5]

Babies play with the sounds of words. Young children delight in rhyme, revelling in the fact that one word sounds like another. All poetry — indeed, all writing — is a kind of word play: [10] slotting words into appropriate (or inappropriate) places, shifting words around like the pieces of a jigsaw puzzle and choosing those that make up a particular pattern . . . .

. . . Word games may seem trivial but they [15] reflect some truths about humanity. The same impulse which drives poets, playwrights and artists also moves us to play with words: to find order in what we are given, to make new sense (or nonsense) by playing with the basic [20] elements of our language, as well as for pure entertainment and enjoyment. Word games can never compete with the arts but perhaps they are the foothills of literature, involving the same sort of creativity, although at a [25] humbler, more approachable level.

Text 3

Catch-22

The phrase 'catch-22' comes from Joseph Heller's famous book of that name. In that book a fighter pilot asked to be excused flying duties on the grounds that he was insane. Since flying under the particular [5] conditions involved in the book was regarded as highly dangerous, this request showed signs of sanity, and he was therefore refused permission to be grounded. In other words if a pilot was sane enough not to want [10] to fly, then he could not be excused flying on the grounds of insanity.

If one looks around there are any number of catch-22 situations. Television producers are always crying out for new ideas but if the [15] idea is really new they will not be able to tell from past experience whether it will work. So they say: 'Give us a new idea but if it is really new then we shall be unable to use it.'

b Read the texts again quickly and answer the questions below in pairs or groups.

1 How many of the writers talk about babies?

2 What do word games reveal?

3 What happens around the age of eighteen months?

4 What do babies play with?

5 Who wrote Catch-22?

c What kind of text is each extract from? Choose from this list and explain the reasons for your choice in pairs or groups.

a dictionary   a novel
an introduction to a book
a manual about bringing up children
a book about the English language
a book about new words
a book about the human brain

d Answer the following questions.

1 What's the difference between 'all gone' and 'Daddy come'?

2 What kinds of people play with words and language?

3 Can you explain simply what a 'catch-22 situation' is?

1.3) Vocabulary

a With a partner, match the 'word' idioms on the left with the definitions on the right. The first one has been done as an example.

1 to have the final word	**a** to speak on somebody's behalf, to support or defend somebody
2 in other words	**b** by speaking and not by writing
3 I give you my word	**c** to make the final decision
4 to put in a good word for somebody	**d** to admit to being wrong
5 I don't believe a word of it!	**e** to be so amazed, shocked or moved by something that you do not know what to say
6 to eat your words	**f** I promise
7 by word of mouth	**g** something you disapprove of
8 a dirty word	**h** to speak to somebody privately about a delicate matter
9 to have a word in somebody's ear	**i** to express the same thing in different words
10 lost for words	**j** I don't believe it at all

b Listen to the dialogues and check your answers.

c Work in groups. For each of the ten idioms, decide what you would say in your own languages.

1.4) Grammar – articles

a Look at the texts below and complete them using a definite (*the*), indefinite (*a/an*) or zero article.

In most dictionaries, ... (1) words at the top, above the text, tell you the first and last words on those two pages.

Learning .... (2) foreign language is like learning to play .... (3) guitar. We have to recognise new sounds and learn how to make them. At first, ... (4) biggest problem is that our fingers, just like our tongues, can't get the new positions right!

Over 5000 years ago, there was .... (5) language which later developed into many of those spoken in .... (6) world today, including German, English, Spanish, Greek, Russian and many Indian languages. Experts call .... (7) language *Proto-Indo-European*.

At what age does .... (8) child learn to speak? .... (9) parents usually hear .... (10) first word at about one year, and strings of words appear at about eighteen months. But .... (11) grammar develops slowly, continuing after children start .... (12) school, and passive forms are still difficult until about nine years of age.

b Complete the rules using the words below.

again   any   countable   first   general
musical instrument   places   plural
singular   specific   uncountable   unique
unknown   unless

A   A .... , ... noun usually needs an article, either definite (*the*) or indefinite (*a/an*).

B   .... we are talking about a specific thing, we usually use *a/an*:
Can you lend me a pen? This means any pen.
She wants to be an English teacher. There are lots of English teachers.

C   .... and .... nouns need either a definite or zero article.

D   When something is mentioned for the .... time and is .... to the listener/reader because it could be any one of many things, we usually use:
– *a/an* with singular, countable nouns.
– *some* with plural and uncountable nouns.

E   When we mention the thing or things .... , we use *the* because now it is known what is being referred to.

F   It might be obvious for other reasons which specific thing is being referred to, for instance it might be the only one there is, e.g. *the sun*. We usually use *the* with things that are ....

G   We could give extra information to make it clear which .... thing or things we are talking about, *the books on the table*.

H   When we are speaking about something .... , we often use a zero article, e.g. *love is a wonderful thing – cats hate swimming*.

I   We sometimes use a singular noun with a general meaning, e.g. *a mother loves her children* meaning .... mother or all mothers.

J   When we talk about playing a .... , we say *the piano* even though we don't mean a specific one.

K   With certain .... , like school, hospital, university, prison and church, we don't use articles when talking about their normal uses: *criminals go to prison* but *their friends visit the prison.*

c Now decide which articles from part a are examples of which rules. Write the numbers of the articles from part a with the correct rule.

A ☐☐☐☐☐☐☐☐
B ☐☐
C ☐☐☐
D ☐
E ☐
F ☐☐☐
G ☐
H ☐☐
I ☐☐
J ☐
K ☐

d Use the rules to make eleven corrections to the following passage.

How many words does English speaker know? This is the difficult question to answer. For one thing, total will vary from one person to another: it is obvious that scientist will probably know many more words – especially the technical terms – than road sweeper. There was, for example, story in media recently saying that someone who has just left the school 'knows' 10 – 12,000 words, but it was clear that a story was not based on research.

Furthermore, what do we mean by 'knowing a word?' The people are able to recognise far more words than they actually use – so do you count the words they recognise or the words they use?

1.5 Conjunctions

One of the most common ways of connecting ideas and sentences together is by using conjunctions. Look at these examples from the texts in 1.2.

*True word-joining, such as 'Daddy come', begins around the age of eighteen months, **although** it may occur later …* (Text 1, line 21)

*Word games may seem trivial **but** they reflect some truths about humanity.* (Text 2, line 15)

***So** they say: 'Give us a new idea **but** if it is really new then we shall be unable to use it.'* (Text 3, line 18)

Conjunctions can be used for different purposes or functions.

The five most common functions are:

1   to give extra information – for example by using **and**;

2   to express contrast – for example by using **but**;

3   to express purpose – for example by using **to + verb**;

4   to express result – for example by using **so**;

5   to express reason – for example by using **because**.

a   Use one sentence start from Column A, one conjunction from Column B, and one sentence end from Column C in the table to form ten full sentences or mini-texts. Use the meaning, the grammar and the punctuation to help you. The first one has been done as an example.

Column A	Column B	Column C
1 He passed the examination	despite	it is full of French and German and Indian vocabulary.
2 The book was easy to understand	so as not to	when they first visit the country where the language is spoken, they find they cannot understand a word!
3 English has very few verb forms	as a result	speaking three languages.
4 He decided to learn Russian	However,	being written in a strange dialect.
5 She has a teaching qualification	whereas	he had not studied very hard.
6 English has always been receptive to words from other languages and	in order to	the large numbers of ethnic minorities living there.
7 A good dictionary will, of course, provide clear definitions of words.	because of	get a job in Siberia.
8 Many people take intensive language courses at home.	as well as	offend disadvantaged groups and minorities.
9 In many British towns you will find a thriving cultural mix	although	it should give grammatical information about them.
10 It has become commonplace to avoid certain expressions such as 'mentally handicapped'	In addition,	some other languages have hundreds!

b Which of the five common functions does each of the ten conjunctions have?

c Look at the ten sentences. For each one, can you think of any other conjunctions which could replace it with exactly the same meaning?

d Finish the following sentences in an appropriate way.

1 Britain is a monarchy, whereas …

2 The house had six bedrooms, two bathrooms and a library as well as …

3 It is a beautifully written novel, although …

4 It rained every day for six weeks and as a result …

5 We arrived late at the airport because of …

6 We carried the birds' eggs in special cartons so as not to …

7 The company has always been very pleased with your work. However …

8 Despite being only 1 metre 46 tall, …

9 She changed her job in order to …

10 I hated New York: there was so much traffic and in addition …

1.6 Learner training

a It is important to store new vocabulary in interesting and memorable ways. Here are three ideas for organising your word-store.

1 ARROWED CIRCLES. These are especially good for collocations (see the Starter Unit page 11).

Decide what the missing word in the middle of the circle is.

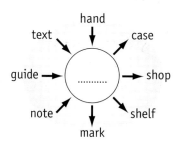

Draw the arrows pointing in the correct direction.

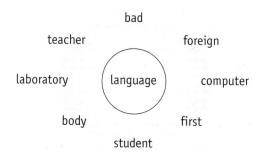

Add more words that collocate with *make.*

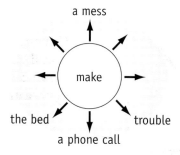

Create your own arrowed circle.

2 SCALES. These are very useful for showing visually how connected words differ from each other without the need to translate them at all.

Look at these adjectives connected with *wet* and *dry.*

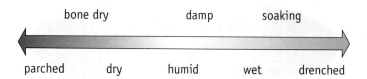

bone dry   damp   soaking

parched   dry   humid   wet   drenched

Now create a scale using the words in the bubble below.

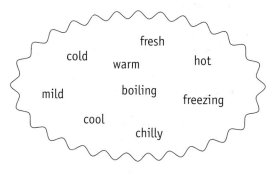

fresh
cold   warm   hot
mild   boiling   freezing
cool
chilly

Scales can also show how words of the same or similar meaning differ in formality.

nosh grub   food   sustenance

INFORMAL   FORMAL

Now create a scale using the words in the bubble below.

sozzled
inebriated   plastered
drunk

3 UNUSUAL, NON-TRADITIONAL GROUPINGS. With these methods of recording vocabulary, you may have different ideas from other students about where to put words or how to classify them, but don't worry: you can discuss your different ideas and, in doing so, learn more about the new vocabulary!

Look at the examples below and add words of your own in each case.

ANIMALS

PETS

cat

dog

horse

tiger   sheep

WILD ANIMALS   FARM ANIMALS

FOOD AND DRINK

Good for you	It depends	Bad for you
apples	wine	chips

CLOTHES

On a mountain	On the beach	To a wedding
gloves	flip-flops	bow-tie

b Start your own word-store. How will you store the vocabulary you have met? Make sure you include some of the techniques in part a.

1.7 Writing – using discourse markers

As we saw in section SU.6, it is important to connect your writing together in a logical and comprehensible way. One way of doing this is by using **discourse markers**. These are words and phrases like *firstly*, *secondly*, *in conclusion* etc. which help the reader to understand the ideas in the text.

a Read the following text and put the discourse markers from the box into the spaces. Some of the words and phrases may go into more than one space. The first one has been done for you as an example.

> as we said above   finally   for example   on the other hand
> to sum up   secondly   an example of this   ~~firstly~~   for instance

The differences between speech and writing are more than just the fact that speech uses the air, and writing is a series of marks on a piece of paper. They are very much independent means of communication.

1 *Firstly* , speech is essentially an interactive, face-to-face process, and participants can rely on 'non-linguistic cues' to help them. **2** *e.g / instance* , if you're talking to somebody, and they're frowning with incomprehension, you'll probably rephrase what you're saying in some way.

3 *On the other h* , if they are nodding furiously, you would probably assume they understand and agree.

4 *Secondly* , because speech is fast and spontaneous, it is quite difficult to plan in advance what you're going to say. This means that speakers often have to go back and rephrase what they've just said, they repeat things, and the construction of the sentences is much looser. (**5** *for ex. / instance* , it is very common for speakers to use long sentences simply joined up with the word *and*.)

6 *Finally* , you can add meaning to what you say by means of things like stress and intonation. **7** *An example of* is making your voice go up at the end of a phrase to indicate you want to carry on talking.

8 *To sum up* , speech and writing display a number of important differences, and, **9** *As we said* , are to be seen as essentially separate mediums.

b Answer these questions.

1 Which expression is used to introduce the first item in a list? And the second? And the last? *Firstly /2nd / lastly*

2 Which three expressions introduce an example of something? *For example / for instance*

3 Which expression introduces a contrast? *On the other*

4 Which expression introduces something you have already said earlier in the text?

5 Which expression starts a concluding sentence or paragraph?

6 What is the purpose of these expressions (in general)? Do you think they succeed in this purpose?

c Imagine a friend is learning English, and has asked you for advice on how to learn and remember vocabulary. Using the information about storing vocabulary in 1.6, and any ideas of your own, write a reply. Use the discourse markers in the section above.

1.8 Writing – punctuation

In all writing, it is very important to check your work carefully once you have finished it. Read the following paragraph and punctuate it correctly.

Crosswords

the man generally credited with inventing the crossword puzzle was a journalist named arthur wynne who emigrated to new york from liverpool his first crossword appeared in a sunday newspaper
5 the new york world on 21 december 1913 wynne called it a word-cross the puzzle had the word fun near the top because it appeared on the fun page of the newspaper the shape resembled a word diamond but the across words differed from the down words
10 readers expressed their approval of the experiment so wynne devised further puzzles for the paper by the middle of january the name had changed from word-cross to cross-word readers began to contribute their own crosswords

---

1.9 Pronunciation – word stress

It is important to stress a word in the right place. Sometimes this is more important than the individual sounds. For example, if you said the word **palace** with the stress on the second half, it would sound like **place**.

a Think about where the stress comes in the following words.

photograph   photographer   photographic

In a dictionary, the stress is usually marked by the sign ` before the stressed syllable.

---

pho·to·graph
(obj) /£ˌfəʊ·tə·grɑːf, $ˈfoʊ·toʊ·græf/ v •
I prefer photographing people rather than places.
[T] • *MacKay was photographed leav**ing** the build-ing.* [T + obj + v + ing] • You can say that a person photographs **well/badly**, meaning that he or she appears attractive/unattractive in photographs. [I always + adv]

pho·tog·raph·er
/£fə'tɒg·rə·fə, $-'tɑː·grə·fə/ n [C] • A pho-tographer is a person who takes photographs, either as a job or a hobby: *a fashion/press/ama-teur photographer* • *a keen/good photographer.*

pho·to·graph·ic
/£ˌfəʊ·tə'græf·ɪk, $ˌfoʊ·tə-/ adj [not grad-able] • *photographic equipment/film/materials* • *pho-tographic skills* • *There is a system which allows you to store up to 100 photographic **images** on a CD and watch them on a television or computer screen.* • *The agreement forbids the photographic **reproduction** of written, printed, or graphic work.* • *Her paintings are almost photographic in their detail and accuracy.* • If you have a **photographic memory** you are able to remember things in exact detail.

When you record new words, the simplest way to note the stress is with a big bubble over the main stressed syllable and smaller bubbles over the other syllables:

◯ ○ ○   ○ ◯ ○ ○   ○ ○ ◯ ○
photograph   photographer   photographic

b Try to guess where the stress comes in these words. Mark it by putting a big bubble over the main stressed syllable and small bubbles above the other syllables. The first one has been done as an example.

○ O ○ ○
photographer   gestures

average   characteristics

apparently   particular

situations   delight

constantly   dangerous

applied   existence

alternatively   creativity

appropriate   frivolous

c Now listen to the tape and check your answers.

d Work in pairs. One of you should follow the instructions below for Student A, while the other does the same for Student B.

STUDENT A
Look at the words in List A. Turn to page 75, where the list is printed with the words marked with stress bubbles. Using these as your guide, read out the words to Student B, who will mark the stress.

Then listen to Student B reading List B, and mark the stress on those words, by putting a big bubble over the main stressed syllable, and small circles over the others, as above.

STUDENT B
Look at List A. Student A will read out the words to you with the correct stress. Mark the stress on the words, by putting a big bubble over the main stressed syllable and small circles over the others, as above.

Then look at List B. Turn to page 122 where the list is printed with the words marked with stress bubbles. Using these as your guide, read out the words to Student B, who will mark the stress.

LIST A

humanity

language

expression

entertainment

communication

request

business

lovable

animal

although

LIST B

pilot

literature

associates

regarded

excused

reproduces

character

devise

jigsaw

enjoyment

Now check your pronunciation by listening to the tape.

2

Healthy mind, healthy body

(2.1) To start you thinking

a Work in pairs. Discuss the following questions with your partner.

1 Would you describe yourself as healthy, not very healthy or totally unhealthy?

2 Which parts of your lifestyle and routine are good or bad for you?

b In groups of three or four, categorise the following factors into those which you think are important for physical health, for mental health and for both.

exercise   diet   being married
bad habits   temperament   stress
environment   self-esteem   owning a pet
heredity   children   laughter   crying
living alone   money   love

2.2) Reading

a Skim through the following **five** articles. Which article(s) would be of interest to the following people:

a comedian   a skin specialist   a dietician   a trainee surgeon
someone worried about not being fit enough

An electric heart powered by two rechargeable batteries worn on a belt is the latest thing in artificial organs. Made of titanium, the grapefruit-sized heart is inserted inside the wall of the abdomen and connected to the old heart by two tubes. It then collects freshly oxygenated blood from the old heart and pumps it round the body, allowing 500 patients around the world to lead a virtually normal life without having a transplant. 'Heart failure is the greatest killer of people over 60 and, as we have an ageing population, it's going to be the health epidemic of the future,' says Stephen Westaby, a cardiac surgeon at John Radcliffe Hospital, Oxford, who performed the operation on a volunteer last November. 'New types of artificial hearts could be in routine use within the next five years.' An artificial pump the size of a thumbnail is also being developed for use in children.

Article 1

Moderate exercise may make you healthier, but living longer calls for something more strenuous, says a new report.

The study by Harvard School of Public Health, which followed 17,321 male Harvard graduates for more than 20 years, shows that only vigorous activity reduces the risk of dying early.

Scientists revealed in the Journal of the American Medical Association that participants who reported burning off at least 1,500 calories a week in vigorous exercise had up to a 25% reduced death rate compared with those expending less than 150 a week. The researchers suggest that the benefits come from better functioning of the heart and lungs.

Article 2

Article 3

Those of us who doze our way through life have always been the target of mountebanks and quacks. Today there are endless mind foods, smart drugs, potions and compounds available to counter the unwelcome side effects of life. Some, of course, work only because we want them to work. Suggestibility is a vital part of the healing process.

But others show signs of increasing popularity and acceptance. Their existence on the border between food and medicine has given rise to their new catch-all handle 'nutriceuticals'.

At Charing Cross Hospital in West London, for example, the appearance of lively cocktail waiters on the cancer wards has done much to improve patients' daily nutritional intake.

Patients get a welcome opportunity to engage with the volunteers who run the service on a light-hearted level that is, frankly, fun. The cocktails are made from a variety of nutriceutical food supplements, fruit juices and yogurt. This is the only food some patients can take.

In the commercial market, there are items such as *Kombucha*, a naturally fermented elixir of what the French call le champignon de longue vie. It is full of the amino-acids of which we ourselves are composed – and has a taste that compares favourably to a light sparkling Moselle. Obtain a *Kombucha* 'mother' (like a ginger beer 'plant'), look after it well, and drink the liquor to keep your metabolism well-tuned and the effects of age at bay.

Article 4

Certain foods and drugs have the alarming side effect of turning your skin a different colour. For example, scoffing too many tangerines and satsumas, resulting in an excess of beta-carotene, can produce an orange hue to the skin that's particularly noticeable on the palms of the hands and soles of the feet. And no fewer than 22 listed medicines can oxidise the iron in the blood, causing the bewildered patient literally to turn blue.

You stagger down to the doctor. Stressed-out by the pressures of modern life, you are plagued by a host of minor symptoms. The twinge of pain in your lower back just won't go away, you can't shake off that cough and you feel constantly tired. Your GP listens carefully, scribbles a few notes and hands over the prescription: 'Take regular doses of laughter and come and see me again in a fortnight.'

This scenario may sound far-fetched, but laughter medicine is one of the fastest growing branches of modern healthcare. Over 500 scientific papers have been published about its physiological and psychological benefits and three years ago treatment became available on prescription in Britain's first laughter clinic. Fun therapy is big news.

'Modern medicine, accused of being over-technical and over-preoccupied with illness, is showing a willingness to explore the medicinal role of emotions, touch and laughter,' says stress consultant Robert Holden, who set up the Laughter Clinic in Birmingham.

As well as helping to deepen breathing, laughter regulates our heartbeat, balances our blood pressure and calms the muscles. When a smile turns into a body-rocking laugh, our facial muscles crease, which in turn stimulates the underlying blood vessels to the brain, so increasing flow.

Article 5

b Now read the articles again quickly (maximum two minutes for all five articles) and decide which one talks about the following:

1 the relationship between food and skin colour;

2 the relationship between health and what we eat;

3 exercise and living longer;

4 a new artificial organ;

5 why smiling is good for you.

c For each article, decide which of the three points listed is the **main** point and which are the **subsidiary** points.

Article 1
1 heart failure kills more people over 60 than any other disease
2 a new electronic heart has been developed
3 artificial heart pumps will soon be available for children

Article 2
1 if you want to live longer, you have to take very vigorous exercise
2 moderate exercise makes you healthier
3 if you burn off at least 1,500 calories per week, your heart and lungs will work better

Article 3
1 many drugs and potions only work because we want them to work
2 lively cocktail waiters have helped patients eat more in one London hospital
3 there are now lots of new health-giving foods and drinks available called nutriceuticals

Article 4
1 if you go blue, it may be because of the medicine you are taking
2 tangerines and satsumas turn your skin orange
3 you can change colour if you eat too much of certain foods

Article 5
1 Britain's first laughter clinic has opened in Birmingham
2 modern medicine has become too technical
3 doctors are realising that laughter can cure many things

d Suggest a title for each of the articles.

(2.3) Collocations

a Refer to the articles on pages 25 and 26 to complete the collocations below. An alternative is given in brackets to help you.

Article 1
1 is the ....*latest*.... (most recent) thing
2 to .... (have) a normal life
3 freshly .... (aerated) blood
4 a health .... (widespread problem)

Article 2
5 to .... (use) calories
6 .... (light) exercise
7 .... (hard) exercise

Article 3

8   to .... (block) unwelcome side effects

9   the .... (repairing) process

10   a new catch-all .... (name)

11   to keep the side effects of age .... (away)

Article 4

12   .... (very surprising/ worrying) side effects

13   produce an orange .... (colour) to the skin

Article 5

14   a .... (small amount) of pain

15   to .... (get rid of) a cough

16   take regular .... (quantities)

17   treatment available .... (as ordered by your doctor)

18   a host of minor .... (signs of illness)

b Look at the following noun + noun collocations, which are all to do with health and medicine, and put them in one of these four categories. The first four are shown as examples.

1   Medical problems: heart failure

2   People who help you with a problem: cardiac surgeon

3   Treatments: painkillers

4   Other: first aid box

~~heart failure~~	~~cardiac surgeon~~
~~painkillers~~	~~first aid box~~
side effects	life-support machine
healthcare	stress consultant
heartbeat	metabolic rate
cancer ward	food supplements
eye test	cholesterol levels
plastic surgery	low-fat diet
flu jab	General Practitioner
blood clot	high blood pressure

c Complete the sentences below with collocations from part b.

1   We had a serious flu ...._epidemic_.... last year and had to close the school for two weeks.

2   One of the possible .... of the new drug is hair loss.

3   They refused to let me buy the pills over the counter as they said they were only available ....

4   Any .... should contain bandages and dressing as an absolute minimum.

5   I've had a cold for ages and I just can't .... it ....

6   Laura suffers from severe backache and has to take .... most days.

7   Some people with a high .... can eat whatever they like without getting fat.

8   Daniel was so seriously injured that he had to be kept alive on a ....

9   I've recovered more or less now except for a few .... of pain in my legs.

10   Surprisingly enough, digging the garden is one of the best ways of .... excess calories!

2.4 Grammar – review of futures

a Read the medical students' conversation and decide where it is possible to use will. If will is not possible, choose another future form.

LIZ: Kate's finished her case study already! She's asked her friend to type it and she'll meet (1) her this evening. I'm still working on mine – have you finished yours yet?

SIMON: Finished? I've not even started.

LIZ: What! Term will start (2) on Monday, you know. Which patient will you write about (3)?

SIMON: I'm not sure, I will look (4) at Mr West's liver trouble, or I will do (5) Mrs Chung's blood condition, or … Oh, I don't know …

LIZ: I know I'll never finish (6) mine in time, so I've thought it over and I'll ask (7) Dr Wheeler for an extension on the deadline.

SIMON: Really? I know! I'll do (8) the same!

b Write the name of the tense/verb forms with a future meaning in the list 1–12 below, then match the sentence with the correct description of use from the list a–l.

Example sentence	Description of use
1 I'm seeing the doctor at 3.00. I've made an appointment. _Present Continuous_	a Action already completed by a future point in time.
2 We might/may go to a health farm next month.	b Action around a future point in time.
3 The lectures on food hygiene start on the 17th.	c Duration of an incomplete action up to a future point in time.
4 I'm going to visit the Science Museum this weekend.	d Established arrangement, usually organised with other people.
5 He'll fail the medical.	e Future event determined by a timetable.
6 Quick, give me a tissue. I'm going to sneeze.	f Intention, not yet arranged.
7 No, don't ring at 1.30. I'll be having lunch.	g Possible plan, with some indication of degree of probability.
8 They say they'll have finished the new hospital by next summer.	h Prediction of something seen as certain.
9 She'll have been writing that book for a year this time next month.	i Prediction of something seen as uncertain, with some indication of degree of probability.
10 That equipment looks heavy – I'll help you carry it, if you like.	j Simultaneity of two on-going future actions.
11 Her husband's promotion is so ironic. She'll be fighting for higher pay for nurses, and he'll be trying to cut hospital funding!	k Something seen as certain to happen due to strong evidence or because it is already beginning.
12 She might/may not survive the operation.	l Spontaneous decision.

C Complete the sentences with the correct tense/verb form.

1 Daniella's studying medicine – she .... (be) a doctor.

2 Alice, can you remind me that I .... (meet) Dr Kim at the airport this afternoon?

3 Just think, this time next month you .... (work) for Médicins Sans Frontières somewhere in Africa.

4 What time .... the exam .... (start) tomorrow?

5 By this time tomorrow, she .... (have) the operation. Let's just hope there are no complications.

6 Come on, the meeting .... (start) at eight o'clock. It's five to already. We .... (be) late as usual!

7 Personally, I'm convinced there .... (not be) any tooth decay in 50 years' time.

8 Her mother .... (work) at the same clinic for 25 years at the beginning of next month.

9 I'm not sure who else to see about my backache. I thought I .... (try) an acupuncturist, or I .... (visit) an osteopath.

10 The X-rays .... (prove) me wrong, but it looks broken to me.

11 I .... (think) of you while you .... (have) the operation.

12 Don't try to move him! I .... (phone) an ambulance.

 LISTENING

a Answer the following questions.

1 Are you or is anyone you know allergic to any food?

2 What happens when you/they eat it?

3 What do you think is the difference between food allergy and food intolerance?

 b Read the following questions, then listen to a radio interview about people's reactions to food and answer the questions.

1 When did the woman presenter have a reaction to food? *about a year ago*

2 Was it a food allergy or not? *unclear maybe intolerance*

3 What two types of tests can be used to determine if someone has a food allergy? *Skin tests and blood tests*

4 What are IGE? *Antibodies in the blood*

5 Name three foods which most frequently produce an allergy. *Any 3 from milk, eggs, shellfish, fish + peanuts -*

6 Name some of the symptoms produced by food intolerance. *Migraine irritable bowel, aching joints, not feeling well, tiredness*

7 Which of these are people most often intolerant to: bread, alcohol, cheese, potatoes, butter? *bread (wheat + yeast) alcohol, cheese + butter*

yeast = beer.

8 How are people with food intolerance frequently treated by their doctor? *they are often labelled neurotic*

2.6 Pronunciation – weak and strong forms

a **Work in pairs to identify the main verb(s) and the auxiliary verb(s) in the following sentences.**

1 He's been seeing a psychiatrist for two years.

2 Has the doctor examined you yet?

3 What shall we have for supper tonight?

4 It was threatening to become an ugly situation.

5 If we could only find out what the problem is, …

6 The two climbers were injured.

7 There've been six or seven similar accidents in the last two years.

8 What time do they normally do these tests?

9 Did you really believe him?

10 Patients can purchase tea and coffee on level four.

b **Listen to the sentences being read aloud and identify how the main verbs are pronounced and how the auxiliary verbs are pronounced. Do you notice any common differences? How would you describe the way the auxiliary verbs are pronounced?**

c **Practise saying the sentences. Concentrate on saying the main verb correctly – don't worry about the auxiliary verb at the moment.**

d **The following pairs of sentences contain the same auxiliary verb (ignore other auxiliary verbs). In each case, decide if the auxiliary verb is pronounced as a weak form or a strong form. Then listen to the tape and check.**

1 a Can you help me?
  b I'm not sure if you can.

2 a Oh, I do like geraniums!
  b Do you think so?

3 a How many heart attacks has he had?
  b Oh yes he has.

4 a How do you spell 'could'?
  b At what time could you get here?

5 a What on earth were you thinking of?
  b Well, we were going to Ibiza, but at the last moment we decided to go to Blackpool instead.

6 a Where did you go?
  b He said he spoke to her, but I don't know if he really did.

7 a She's living in Manchester now, isn't she?
    She was, but she's moved.
  b There was a man at the bus stop.

8 a Where have you been hiding?
  b Yes, I have.

2.7 Hearing perception

 Follow the instructions given by your teacher.

2.8 Learner training

a **All of the following could be used to answer the question 'How are you feeling?' Put them in the most appropriate area of the circles below. Three ways have been done as an example.**

off colour   full of beans   chuffed

b In pairs, decide how the question 'How are you feeling?' would be answered by someone who …

1 has just passed a fairly difficult exam.

2 is always being criticised by their boss at work.

3 has just come back from a health farm having lost five kilos.

4 has been working twelve hours a day for the last three months.

5 has a headache and a slight temperature.

6 has not been offered a new job they thought they would get.

7 has a migraine and stomach ache and who has been vomiting for twelve hours.

8 has just won a lot of money on the lottery.

9 didn't get a good night's sleep because their neighbours were having a party.

10 has been anxiously waiting for the results of some medical tests for over a week.

2.9 Writing – brainstorming for ideas

a Imagine you have been asked to write a magazine article explaining what habits and styles of everyday life might lead to good health. You think for about ten minutes and write the following ideas in your notepad.

> NO smoking   lots of exercise – esp. swimming
> diet – lots of fresh fruit & veg
> fish good – red meat bad
> grill – not fry
> don't drink too much alcohol   avoid stress
> live in the country   reduce caffeine intake
> walk/cycle – use the car as little as poss.
> don't live on your own (get married = best!)

Are there any other notes you would like to add?

b In groups of three or four, decide how to organise the notes above into paragraphs. You decide how many paragraphs to have (probably no more than five). Try to put similar ideas into the same paragraph.

c Write the article based on the paragraphs you have prepared.

2.10 Review

Complete the following story with words you studied in Unit 1.

I'll never forget meeting my 'friend' Jack in ………… (1) street one day. I told him I had applied for ………… (2) job in his company and that I thought I had a good chance of getting it. As a bit of a joke, I then asked him if he could ………… (3) in a good word for me ………… (4) well. ………… (5) he had been my friend for ages, Jack said he wouldn't, so ………… (6) not to 'compromise his position'.

Anyway, I got the job ………… (7) Jack's refusal to help me!

Five years later, I had moved to another company and been promoted. One day, I learnt by word of ………… (8) that Jack had applied for a job in the same company and wanted to know if I could help him make a good impression. I really should have made him ………… (9) his pompous words of five years earlier! In the end, ………… (10), I decided to mention his good qualities to the boss.

Now we're workmates and the best of friends again.

Getting away from it all

3.1 To start you thinking

Look quickly through the questions below. Then, when you're ready, form a group of three or four and talk about your answers.

1 What's the first holiday you remember – how old were you, where did you go, did you enjoy it?

2 When did you first go on holiday without your family?

3 Where's the best place you've ever been in your country (and why did you like it)?

4 Where's the best place you've been abroad (and why did you like it)?

5 What's the longest journey you've ever made?

6 Where would you most like to go? Why?

3.2 Discussion

a Write down three items (apart from passport, money and clothes) which you think are **essential** when you're on holiday abroad.

b Compare your list with other students and explain why you think your items are so important.

3.3 Reading

a Five people whose lives revolve around travelling were asked to think of one indispensable item without which they never leave home. Match each person's letter (A – E) with the answer you think they gave.

A Cathy Wood, travel correspondent for the *Daily Mail*.

B Sir Ranulph Fiennes, Arctic explorer.

C Alan Whicker, reporter for TV and radio travel programmes.

D Caroline Brandenburger, editor of *The Traveller* magazine.

E Kate Moss, supermodel.

b When you have decided, compare your answers in pairs or groups and explain what helped you make your choices.

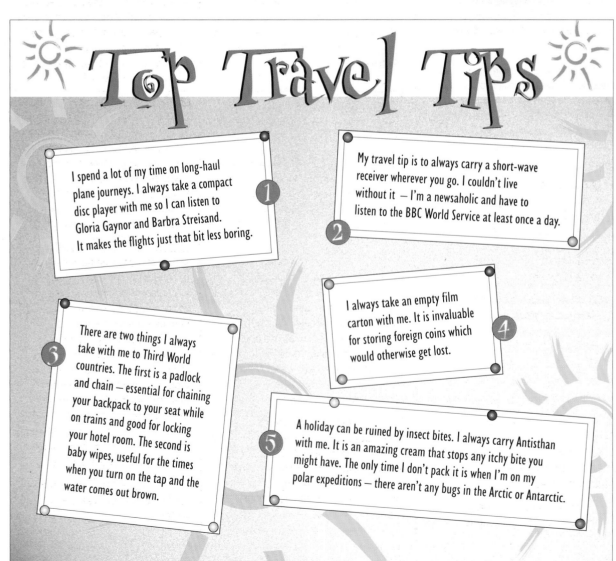

Top Travel Tips

1 I spend a lot of my time on long-haul plane journeys. I always take a compact disc player with me so I can listen to Gloria Gaynor and Barbra Streisand. It makes the flights just that bit less boring.

2 My travel tip is to always carry a short-wave receiver wherever you go. I couldn't live without it — I'm a newsaholic and have to listen to the BBC World Service at least once a day.

4 I always take an empty film carton with me. It is invaluable for storing foreign coins which would otherwise get lost.

6 There are two things I always take with me to Third World countries. The first is a padlock and chain — essential for chaining your backpack to your seat while on trains and good for locking your hotel room. The second is baby wipes, useful for the times when you turn on the tap and the water comes out brown.

5 A holiday can be ruined by insect bites. I always carry Antisthan with me. It is an amazing cream that stops any itchy bite you might have. The only time I don't pack it is when I'm on my polar expeditions — there aren't any bugs in the Arctic or Antarctic.

3.4 Reading

a The following passage is a humorous article on the more unpleasant aspects of holidays and travelling. Scan the article quickly to find the answers to the following questions.

1 Is the writer a man or a woman?

2 Where does s/he live?

3 Is s/he helpful to foreign tourists or not?

4 Who does s/he prefer to go on holiday with?

5 Does s/he usually go on holiday with this person?

6 What does his/her partner love eating while on holiday?

7 How does his/her partner order this food when abroad?

8 What did the writer learn to do to avoid this embarrassing problem?

DO I WANT TO GET AWAY FROM IT ALL?

GIVE ME A BREAK ...

There is nothing I don't know about miserable holidays. I'm either on one, hearing about one or, more often than not, watching one unfold from the comfort of my living room window. 5

My neighbourhood is full of budget hotels which heave every month with package tourists from all over the world. Every day, you can find me happily absorbed, twitching my curtains and enjoying the show. 10

Until they knocked down the hotel over the road, a coach would pull up outside daily and disgorge dozens 15 of tourists. One glimpse down our street, with its peeling stucco and abandoned shopping trolleys, and you could see them already wishing they were back home. 20

I watch them leave in the morning to see the sights, always in their holiday uniforms of shiny tracksuits lashed with money bags, their big feet encased in squashy white 25 trainers. I see them come back at night, looking exhausted and fed up, their shoes scuffed with grime, the mums and dads no longer speaking to each other. Local 30 residents are always being asked to take photographs of them outside their cheesy hotels.

The holiday-makers are always stopping locals to ask directions 35 to the Albert Hall or Windsor Castle, and I always give them information with excessive jollity because it breaks my heart to see them wandering down Cromwell Road, 40 looking so disappointed not to be in Belgravia or Chelsea. I know I am not giving a good impression of Britain – gabbling away like mad, laughing at my own jokes, wearing 45 jim-jams in the street – but at least I try.

A ＿＿＿＿＿ when it comes to holidays, anticipation and happy memories are key parts. The worst 50 bit is the awful period in the middle when you actually have to go away somewhere.

B ＿＿＿＿＿ I vowed to myself that I would never go on 55 holiday with a partner again, and stick to vacationing with my girlfriends. At least with your pal you can relax every once in a while, knowing that she will take her turn 60 to go fetch the occasional Pina Colada and help tidy up your rented cabin now and then.

She will not stand in the middle of the room every morning, peer 65 hopelessly into a jumbled suitcase and say: 'Where are my blue socks?' She will not start freaking out because she cannot find her lucky vest. 70

C ＿＿＿＿＿ and I have been on many holidays with my sweetheart. Over the past two years we have trailed across France, Italy and Spain every autumn in pursuit 75 of the one thing – apart from me – that can make his heart beat a little faster: a plate of wild boar.

D ＿＿＿＿＿ I can't stand the stuff – it's like eating a nugget 80 of steak from a cow which smoked too many cigars – but I would like to thank him sincerely for my increased knowledge of Spanish, French and Italian. I now know how to say: 85 'Hello, patron! Do you have any wild boar on the menu today?'

E ＿＿＿＿＿ I could no longer stand the embarrassment of him performing his wild boar 90 impersonation – index fingers aloft at either side of nose, loud honking sounds – each time he tried to explain his culinary desire to a waiter. In one restaurant in Italy, 95 after just such a performance, the waiter beamed delightedly when comprehension finally dawned. 'Ah si, si!' he exclaimed. And then he went off to put a George Michael 100 tape on the sound system, happily waggling the box in our direction.

F ＿＿＿＿＿ happy holidays everyone. It's back to the window for me. 105

b Now read the article more carefully, and choose the most appropriate word or phrase for each of the gaps A – F. Be careful, there are more phrases than gaps!

1 Promises, however, are made to be broken

2 The point of all this is that

3 Actually, to be honest,

4 So,

5 Naturally enough,

6 Years ago,

7 This is only because

8 As a result,

3.5) Vocabulary

a There are some words in 3.4 that you have probably never seen before. Working in pairs, without a dictionary, find the following words in context and deduce their meaning.

1 twitching (line 11)

2 cheesy (line 33)

3 jollity (line 38)

4 gabbling away (line 44)

5 jim-jams (line 46)

6 vowed (line 54)

7 pal (line 58)

8 jumbled (line 66)

9 freaking out (line 68)

10 sweetheart (line 73)

11 honking (line 92)

12 beamed (line 97)

b Now compare your answers with other pairs. Give reasons for your decisions.

3.6) Reading

Read through the following descriptions and decide which country is being described.

Choose from the places in the box below (there are more places than descriptions). Note down the words or phrases which help you decide.

India	Australia	Japan	Costa Rica
Brazil	New Zealand	China	Greece

① A staggering array of history, natural beauty and friendly people, a journey to .... remains one of the world's most enticing and enigmatic experiences, likely to be enjoyed more by the traveller than the tourist. See the legendary Great Wall for a once-in-a-lifetime experience, Xian and its imposing Terracotta Army Warriors, then on to Guilin to cruise the River Li past the spectacular 'Willow Pattern' scenery.

② The south, though less well-known than the Moghul area of the north, is a region of great charm, offering no shortage of beautiful cities and temples and first-class hotels, but in addition you'll find a more relaxed lifestyle, with friendly smiling people and attractive scenery throughout. Gentle forest-clad hills slope down through the palm-fringed rice paddies to a shoreline of shady lagoons and sandy beaches, lapped by the placid blue waters of the Arabian Sea.

③ Staying at one of the many charming, spotlessly clean local hotels gives you the chance to explore the intricate maze of backstreets, the bustling flea markets and the ancient ruins that so inspired Homer and Byron. From there, take an island ferry; Tinos is just 5 hours away. You can relax on secluded beaches, swim in emerald waters or try some energetic watersports. If all-night Ouzo-drinking and disco dancing are more your scene, go to the backpackers' mecca, Santorini, where the days are spent sleeping off the nights!

3.7 Vocabulary

Copy these arrowed circles into your vocabulary notebook and complete them with adjectives from 3.6, all of which are used in holiday brochures to make things sound more impressive or attractive. This exaggerated use of language is known as **hyperbole**.

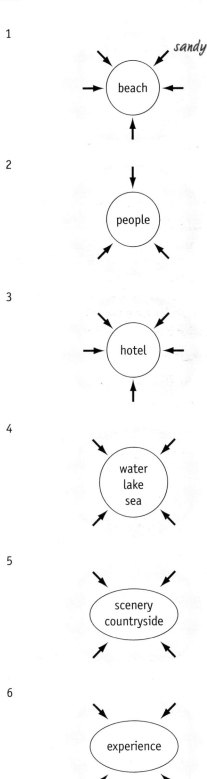

1

sandy

beach

2

people

3

hotel

4

water
lake
sea

5

scenery
countryside

6

experience

4 What a marvellous place! Tranquillity, natural beauty, mighty volcanoes, lakes, rivers, rolling countryside, glorious unspoilt beaches, wildlife, sophisticated hotels, charming people and an agreeable climate. The diversity of this country is mind-boggling, with the Pacific Ocean on one side and the Caribbean on the other. .... also has the third highest standard of living in the Western hemisphere after the USA and Canada.

5 Don't believe what they tell you, there's a lot more to .... than rugby and sheep! Each island displays surprisingly different cultures but they have beautiful beaches, friendly people and lots of sunshine in common. In the lush warm north, there's scuba diving, surfing and cave rafting. In the south, mountaineering and skiing in breathtaking alpine scenery or the never-to-be-forgotten experience of whale-watching in the crystal clear coastal waters. Whatever you choose, you'll always be surrounded by some of the world's most spectacular landscapes.

3.8 Learner training

Using an English-English dictionary, look up the words in **bold** below and complete the useful idioms and phrases connected with travel.

1 People say travel **broadens** the *.mind.* but I'm not so sure that's always true.

2 Amanda's got really **itchy** .... – she's just come back from India and now she wants to go off to South America!

3 That souvenir shop's very expensive. Yes, it's a real **tourist** ....

4 I can't understand people who take loads of baggage with them on holiday. I always **travel** ....

5 Most people don't spend very long in the area, they're just **day**-........... .

6 We stayed at a little guesthouse well off the **beaten** .... , about two miles out of the town.

7 Dave didn't spend any money on transport in the States, he **hitch**- .... all the way!

8 I thought I was getting a free trip on their boat but I soon realised I would have to .... my **passage** by doing the cooking.

9 As we had plenty of time, we left the motorway and took the **scenic** ....

10 If you want a cheap air ticket, you should go to a **bucket** ....

3.9 Writing – formal letter

a When writing a formal letter, it is important to use the correct layout; if you don't, you create a bad impression. Put the following components (1–12) in the correct places (A–L) in the letter below.

D 1 Sunspot Holidays, 101 Old Road, Bridstow BD1 1HD

H 2 Please find enclosed a cheque for the full sum of £1,695. I would be most grateful if you could send me a receipt by return of post.

E 3 Re: Walker – 2-week 'Gold Star Break' 28/8 to 10/9

A 4 32 Ridgeway Road Bridstow BD5 6XD

K 5 *Lindsay Walker*

G 6 In response to your letter of 12th August, I am writing to confirm the booking in the name of L. A. Walker for the all-inclusive package holiday to Rovano in Sileria from 28th August to 10th September.

J 7 Yours faithfully, (OR Yours sincerely,)

I 8 I look forward to hearing from you.

C 9 The Manager (OR Mr(s)/Miss/ Ms F. Bond)

B 10 15th August

F 11 Dear Sir or Madam, (OR Dear Mr(s)/Miss/Ms Bond,)

L 12 LINDSAY WALKER

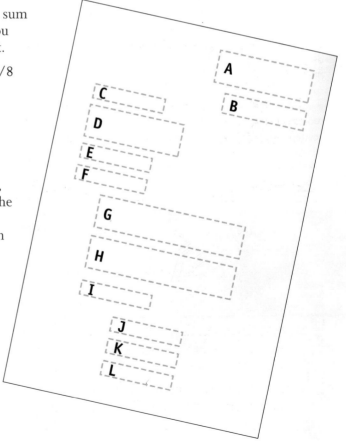

b Based on the notes below about the holiday and the outline letter, write a formal letter of complaint to the travel agency which sold you the holiday and ask for your money back. Remember to be polite at all times!

Nightmare holiday to Rovano 28/8 – 10/9

Flight out – delayed 2 hrs – no explanation. Luggage went to wrong airport → spent first 3 days in same clothes! What a start!

Hotel – brochure stated "the last word in luxury" – not even finished! Builders at work → noisy and dirty. Staff – rude. Food – boring!

Excursions – disorganised! 2 were cancelled!

Resort – brochure stated "an oasis of calm and beauty" – a concrete jungle – cheap shops, tourist flats and discos – very ugly place!

Flight home   8 hr delay! ! ! No explanation!

Absolute disaster – very disappointed – full refund seems reasonable!

Northborough Hill
NW8 ONG St. Johns Wood
London
5th August

The manager
Travel agency

Re: Nightmare holiday to Rovano 28/8 -10/9
Dear Sir or Madam

I am writing to complain in the strongest possible terms about my "Gold Star Break" to Rovano in Sileria from 28th August to 10th September.

First of all, the flight out delayed 2 hrs, without any explanations. Our luggage went to the wrong airport and we spent the first 3 days in same cl.
On arrival, we discovered that the hotel not even finished.
Moreover, we attend the excursions, which were complely disorganised

As for the resort itself, _____

Finally, the return flight delayed 8hrs also without any explanation

All in all, it was an absolute disaster and we are very disappointed, I look forward to recieving a full refund

---

3.10 Grammar – habits and characteristics

a The article in 3.4 contains four typical ways of talking about habits and characteristics. Identify the tense/verb forms used for this in each, and decide if they refer to past, present, future or general time.

Examples	Tense/verb form	Time
1 … I always give them information … (line 37)	always + Present Simple	general time
2 … a coach would pull up outside daily and disgorge dozens of tourists. (line 14)		
3 The holiday-makers are always stopping locals to ask directions … (line 34)		
4 She will not stand in the middle of the room every morning, … (line 64)		

b Read the information, then answer the questions below.

● **The Present Simple** can be used with adverbs like *always* or *usually* to talk about how frequently people do things, and so in some contexts it can describe habits and characteristics. But there are other structures which carry more meaning because they are used specifically to indicate habitual/ characteristic actions and/or states.

● **will** is often used to talk about habits and characteristics. It suggests regular actions that we expect of someone because of past experience of how they act. We don't normally use it with verbs that talk about states, like *be, know, believe, like,* etc. With this meaning, *will* refers to general time not future.

● **The Present Continuous with *always,* *forever* or *constantly*** has a similar meaning to *will* but is stronger, and we tend to use it for actions (not states) which we find irritating and/or surprisingly frequent.

● **The Past Continuous** has the same meaning as the Present Continuous with *always, forever* or *constantly*, but in the past and suggesting that the person doesn't do the action any longer. It is stronger than *would.*

● **would** is used to talk about regular actions (not states) in the past. It usually means that the person doesn't do the action any longer.

● **used to + infinitive** has the same meaning as *would*, but we also use it to talk about states.

1 In part a, which verb form could be replaced by *used to* + infinitive?

2 In one of the sentences below, *would* + verb cannot be used. Which one is wrong and why?

  a Helen would be excellent at Chinese when she worked in Beijing.

  b She would speak Chinese all the time.

3 Correct the underlined mistake in each of the following sentences.

  a My ex-boss had a terrible memory; <u>he's</u> always forgetting his passport.

  b His wife never stops planning her next holiday – <u>she's talking</u> about it.

  c On holidays abroad, my mother's main interest was the restaurants – she <u>would be</u> crazy about foreign food!

C Complete the sentences with the most suitable verb form from the structures used above.

1 I .... (*forget*) clients' names. As a tour leader it's really most embarrassing.

2 On Sundays when I lived in Italy, we .... (*get up*) early in the morning and go skiing.

3 Jenny .... (*get*) bad marks for her French at school until we started going to France for our summer holidays.

4 Our new au pair is an absolute angel, she .... (*help*) the kids with their homework for hours.

5 Frank .... (*have*) a strong American accent but he's more or less lost it now.

6 Her husband .... (*bring*) her a little souvenir whenever he went away on business trips.

7 Dennis hates flying. He .... (*sit*) next to the window unless he really has to.

8 One of the waiters at the hotel .... (*ask*) her to go out with him until she told him to leave her alone.

9 Before the children were born we .... (*go*) camping in the mountains most weekends.

10 People .... (*think*) that the earth was flat!

3.11 Listening

Read the following questions, then listen to this radio extract about an unusual town in Florida and answer the questions.

1 Is the reporter in town A, B or C?

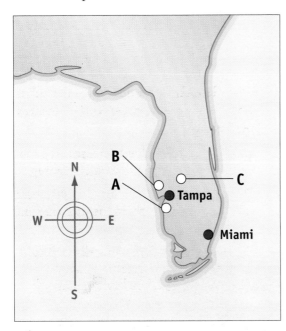

2 Which road did she take from Tampa to Tarpon Springs?

3 Did she enjoy the drive?

4 What building is there in the middle of the town?

5 When does the young man feel confused?

6 What proportion of the population is of Greek origin?

7 Why are the customs of these American Greeks more traditional than those of Greek Greeks?

8 Who gets 'preferential treatment'?

9 What surprises the reporter about the coffee shop?

10 Apart from drinking coffee, what do they do in the coffee shop nowadays?

3.12 Hearing perception

Follow the instructions given by your teacher.

3.13 Pronunciation – elision

In spoken English, when the last sound of a word is the same as, or very similar to, the first sound of a following word, they are not pronounced separately but join to form one sound. This is **elision**.

Examples:

bus stop is / bʌstɒp / not / bʌs / / stɒp /

big car is / bɪka: / not / bɪg / / ka: /

Look at the following examples and cross out the sounds that are not pronounced in normal spoken English. Then listen and practise with the tape.

1 junction nine	6 deep blue
2 hard times	7 half full
3 fresh shrimps	8 gin and tonic
4 find time	9 dark green
5 full length	10 hot dish

3.14 Review

Complete the gaps in the passage with vocabulary from Unit 2. The first letter of each missing word is given to help you.

My friend Alex had been feeling rather off c.......... (1) so he went to see his GP. She asked him a few questions about his lifestyle and ran a few tests. The result was that Alex was l.......... (2) a far from healthy life. He was s.......... (3) -out at work, eating all the wrong food and very inactive. Not only that but h.......... (4) was against him – both his grandfathers had died of heart attacks. Worryingly, his h.......... (5) was already quite fast even when 'resting'. The tests also showed he had quite high c.......... (6) levels in his blood. The GP ordered him to change his diet and start taking v.......... (7) exercise if he wanted to keep the u.......... (8) side effects of his lifestyle and family history at b.......... (9).

Six months into his new lifestyle, Alex is a changed man. He's happy, slim and full of b.......... (10). Let's hope he can keep it up!

Crime
never pays?

To start you thinking

a Answer the following questions.

1 Have you or a member of your family ever been victims of a crime?

2 Did you/they tell the police?

3 Did the police solve the crime and punish the offender(s)?

4 Do you think the police are efficient in your country?

b Now form groups of three or four and talk about your answers.

Reading

Read the following questions, then scan through the passage below and answer the questions.

1 What did the Anglo-Saxons consider a crime to be?

2 What was the original significance of doing something against the *King's Peace*?

3 Who was responsible for catching thieves?

4 What was a *tything*?

5 What was a *moot*?

6 If someone saw a crime, what did he have to do?

7 What is the origin of the word *sheriff*?

8 What was a *posse comitatus*?

The Origins of Policing

In early times Britain was settled by waves of different invaders. Among the last of these were the Anglo-Saxons. When they settled in England they lived in small communities, that is, in villages rather than in towns. They brought their own customs and laws to protect people and their property. According to the Anglo-Saxon custom, if someone broke the law it was not just a crime against the victim, but a crime against the whole community.

The Anglo-Saxon kings expected their people to keep good order, and this they called *keeping the peace*. A crime was an act against the peace, and some of the more serious crimes were said to be against the *King's Peace*. Gradually the idea grew that all crimes were against the King's Peace.

Under Anglo-Saxon rule, it was the duty of the citizens themselves to see that the law was not broken, and if it was, to catch the offenders. All the males in the community between the ages of twelve and sixty were responsible for this duty. They were organised in groups of about ten families and each group was called a *tything*: at their head was a *tythingman*. Each member of the tything was held responsible for the good behaviour of the others. If one member of the tything committed a crime, the others had to catch him and bring him before the court, or the *moot* as the Saxons called it. If they failed to do so, they were all punished, usually by paying a fine. In a way, the tythingman is a very early ancestor of the policeman, because it was his duty to see that the King's Peace was kept. If anyone saw a crime, he raised a *hue and cry* and all men had to join in the chase to catch the criminal, and bring him to trial before the court.

For minor offences, people accused of crimes were brought before the local folk moot. More serious cases went to the *hundred court*, headed by a hundredman or *reeve*, or the *shire court* which came under the shire reeve, or *sheriff* as he came to be known. The sheriff was responsible to the King for the peace of the whole area. In an emergency, the sheriff could call out the *posse comitatus* – all the available men in the shire.

4.3 Discussion

Discuss the following questions in groups.

1 What do you think about involving the community in keeping and enforcing the law?

2 Is the police force in your country seen as part of the community or as a separate group of uniformed officials carrying out orders?

3 What type of organisation do you suppose is represented by the picture and slogans on the right?

"Crime cannot live in a community that cares."

Working together for a Safer Community

4.4 Collocations

Match the words in the first column with those in the second column to form collocations connected with law and order. Then write each one in a sentence showing you understand the meaning.

1	commit	a	the law
2	keep	b	someone down
3	bring	c	dog
4	first time	d	someone red-handed
5	break	e	a crime
6	sniffer	f	chase
7	catch	g	offence
8	escape	h	raid
9	track	i	the peace
10	give	j	offender
11	dawn	k	someone to trial
12	minor	l	prosecution

4.5 Reading

The following article is printed in the wrong order. Read it and, using logic and clues in the text, decide what the original order of the article was. The first paragraph has been done for you as an example.

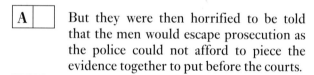

OFFENDERS WEREN'T WORTH PROSECUTING

A ☐ But they were then horrified to be told that the men would escape prosecution as the police could not afford to piece the evidence together to put before the courts.

B ☐ *1* Members of a Neighbourhood Watch scheme have been left fuming after three car thieves they caught red-handed were 'let off'.

C ☐ Other residents called the police and they and Frank later tracked the three men down to where they were hiding in a car in Botley.

D ☐ A police spokesman said: 'It is rather galling when this happens.'

E ☐ Garage owner Frank Green gave chase to three men he saw running off after his BMW's car alarm went off, when its window was smashed outside his home in Meadow Close, Farmoor.

F ☐ Frank said: 'It's a waste of time, isn't it? I was told that as far as the police were concerned they were first time offenders and it wasn't worth putting the evidence together for the judge to say "There's a naughty boy, don't do it again".'

G ☐ Now they are all wondering what the point of Neighbourhood Watch is if criminals they catch just escape with a slapped wrist.

H ☐ 'It's not the police's fault, it's the system that's wrong. As the officer said at the time, there are too many goody-goodies ruling the roost.'

4.6 Writing – achieving formal style

When writing formally, it is important to be clear, well organised and to avoid offending the reader. The following six points will help you achieve the appropriate style.

1 avoid contractions
    e.g. I'm writing → I am writing.

2 choose more formal vocabulary
    e.g. ask → enquire;
          very unhappy → most distressed;
          say → state;
          rude → impolite.

3 use formal linking words
    e.g. and (idea of addition) → moreover, furthermore, what is more;
          but (idea of contrast) → however, on the other hand, whereas;
          so (idea of result) → consequently, as a result, therefore, etc.

4 use passive forms to be more impersonal
    e.g. you still haven't done anything → nothing has been done yet;
          you promised us a discount → a discount was promised;
          you said → it was stated.

5 be indirect
    e.g. it was stupid → it was not very intelligent;
          the service was terrible → the service was somewhat below what one would expect.

6 be tentative (seem, appear, could, would)
    e.g. can you ...? → would it be (at all) possible for you ...?;
          long jail sentences aren't the answer → long jail sentences would not appear to offer a solution;
          fines are no good → fines seem inappropriate.

Jack Brown is writing a letter to Mr Payne, the Chief Constable of Barford. The information in his letter is correct but the style is too informal to create a good impression. Rewrite the letter to make it more formal and include the phrases in the box below.

> I am writing to express my concern about ...
>
> I must insist ...
>
> I must urge you to ...

57 Bath Road
Barford BF8 3DX

Dear Mr Payne,

I'm writing to say just how fed up I am with the number of young criminals and hooligans in my area. Abandoned or vandalised cars everywhere and all the walls covered in graffiti. It's a real mess! Just the other day old Mrs Chilcott, the woman who lives next door, got mugged by some young thug who hit her over the head and nicked her handbag! The poor old thing was really upset by it all.

Now, why have we got all this crime? Well, because the police are a waste of time, of course! They're never on patrol round here and when there is some trouble, they're useless – they just ask a few questions and then go back to the police station!

So, when are you going to do something about it? I think you'd better get some more patrols up here before there's serious trouble. Not only that, when you do arrest one of these little hooligans, you should lock them up for a bit, not just send them home with a telling off – they'll only do it again!

Hoping to hear from you very soon about this problem.

Jack Brown

4.7 Reading

Read the following newspaper article and fill in the gaps with the words in the box. The first one is shown as an example.

> burglaries   recover   sniffer   warrant   ~~net~~   custody   bail   cautioned
> raid   charge   observations   patrols   partnership   officers

Dawn raids net haul of stolen goods

A total of 50 police [2]_____ raided nine houses at dawn, arresting eight people in connection with thefts from supermarkets and [3]_____.

Stolen property was recovered when uniformed CID officers, dog handlers and [4]_____ dogs entered a total of nine premises in Berinsfield early on Monday morning with a [5]_____.

Eight people ranging from 15 to 49 years old were released from police [6]_____ on police [7]_____, and one was charged and bailed for two traffic offences.

Police [8]_____ one of the people for a public order offence and a person was released with no [9]_____ having been arrested to prevent a breach of the peace.

During the [10]_____, police found two cannabis plants, a stolen motor cycle and stolen bicycles.

PC Paul Langford from Didcot police praised the residents who had informed the police of their [11]_____, and the operation was followed up by [12]_____ in the area in the late evening to restore calm to the community.

He said: 'The co-operation of the residents has enabled the police to [13]_____ stolen property and is an excellent example of how the police, working in [14]_____ with the local community, can deal positively with criminal behaviour that has impact on the quality of life for the vast majority of Berinsfield residents.'

4.8 Vocabulary

a Look at the keyword grid below showing words and phrases that are frequently used with the word LAW. Write two short sentences with words from the grid.

Verbs	Describing words	Keyword	Words that come after
break obey bend	criminal civil company	the/a **LAW**	court student abiding citizen

b Now look at the three keyword grids below. Write in the missing keyword and then put words from the bubbles in the correct categories in the grids.

Verbs	Describing words	Keyword	Words that come after
commit	serious	the/a(n)	of passion
arrest	dangerous	the/a(n)	court
call	uniformed	the/a(n)	station

buster   petty   wave
carry out   writer
perfect   investigate

damage   investigation
convict   hardened   record
track down   mind   punish
sentence … to

force   inform   custody
dog   undercover   officer
presence   cooperate with
man/woman   join   car
headquarters   plain-clothes

c Now complete these sentences using some of the vocabulary from the keyword grids above.

1 Her defence was that she had no intention of killing him, it was a ....

2 There's quite a lot of .... in this area, like shoplifting and breaking into cars.

3 They're advertising for more women to .... the police ....

4 .... had infiltrated the gang so they knew exactly who the leaders were.

5 I've heard that if you are arrested, you can be held in .... for up to 48 hours before they charge you.

6 Agatha Christie is probably the world's most famous ....

7 Three bank robberies and fifteen burglaries in just five days – I'd call that a .... !

8 It's very difficult to get a job if your prospective employer knows you've got a ....

9 There was a huge .... at the demonstration.

10 Jones was described as a .... , who showed no compassion for his victims or remorse for his crimes.

4.9 Grammar – reported speech

a Look at the text in boxes 1 and 2. Then read the text in box 3 and complete the sentence in box 4.

1

PC Paul Langford from Didcot police praised the residents who had informed the police.

2 *I must praise the residents who informed the police.*

3 *I was told that as far as the police were concerned they were first time offenders and it wasn't worth putting the evidence together.*

b Read the rules below and underline the words that they refer to in each sentence.

Rules for reported speech:

1 **If the reporting verb is in a past tense, the tense of the actual spoken words usually moves one tense into the past in the reported version.**

   She said she <u>was</u> frightened because she<u>'d seen</u> a burglar, and she <u>was going to lock</u> her windows in future so that she<u>'d be able to get</u> some sleep at night.

2 **Here and now words change according to logic: here becomes there, today becomes that day, last week becomes the previous week, next month becomes the following month, etc.**

   The police claimed that figures published earlier that day showed a big drop in crime in the previous month.

3 **Personal words like pronouns and possessive adjectives change according to logic.**

   The judge told him that if she heard about him battering his wife again, he could expect a prison sentence.

4 **The change in tense does not happen if what was said still remains true.**

   He said he'll pick us up about 2.00.

5 **Reporting verbs are often used to give the general sense of what was said, and so to reduce the number of actual words used.**

   The social worker warned him of the dangers of mixing with other ex-prisoners.

6 **With reported questions, the order of the words usually changes from the question order to the affirmative order.**

   Judy asked where I'd bought the handcuffs and how much they'd cost.

4

They are first time offenders and
.... the evidence together.

4.10 Listening

a Read the following sentences, then listen to a description of a ram-raid by Justin, one of the policemen involved. Put the sentences in the correct order. Don't worry if you don't understand every word.

1 One of the criminals escaped. ☐

2 One of the policemen screamed. ☐

3 Another car almost crashed into the police car. 1

4 The criminals abandoned their car. ☐

5 The two policemen caught two criminals. ☐

6 The fourth man was caught. ☐

7 Justin thought the other criminals would attack him. ☐

8 A second police car arrived on the scene. ☐

c Now look at the reported speech in part b again and write what was actually said, as in the example. Apply all the rules in each sentence.

1 *I'm frightened because I've seen a burglar, and I'm going to lock my windows in future so that I'll be able to get some sleep at night*

d Imagine you are a journalist making notes for your article. Use the rules to report the witnesses' statements.

1 'I'm sure the man was wearing a blue T-shirt,' said the shopkeeper.

2 'It was the same man I saw yesterday when I went to the hairdresser's,' said Mrs Jackson at number 27.

3 'The police never patrol around here any more,' said a passer-by.

4 'I'm not going to tell you anything,' said the bank manager.

b Listen to the description again and decide if the following statements are true or false.

1 Matt's legs were broken.

2 Justin's prisoner did not escape.

3 A police dog fell off a roof.

4 The criminals were sentenced to four years in jail.

5 Justin and Matt received an award for bravery.

4.11 Pronunciation – sentence stress

a Listen again to this short extract from Justin's description and notice which words, or parts of words, he says louder and longer (with stress) and which are weakened (unstressed).

> ∘ O ∘ ∘ OO ∘ ∘ O ∘
> And two of them ran off and were quickly
>
> O ∘ O O O O ∘ ∘ O O
> caught and one ran up on to the roof tops
>
> ∘ ∘ O ∘∘ O O ∘∘ ∘
> and was chased by a dog handler and his
>
> O ∘ O∘ ∘O ∘ O O
> dog, amazingly, on the roof tops …

Stress goes on the words which carry meaning and the words that do not carry meaning are unstressed.

b Now listen to the tape and mark the stressed words (with big bubbles) and unstressed words (with small bubbles) on the following sentences. Then practise saying them correctly.

1. What's your name?
2. How do you do?
3. Do you want a cup of tea?
4. Who's the owner of the car, madam?
5. Has she been working here very long?
6. Janet's gone to the shop to buy some asparagus.
7. Joe wanted to know where I'd hidden the money.
8. Can you tell me the quickest way to the station, please?
9. I was wondering if you could tell me when you last saw your dog.
10. Did you know that John's been arrested on suspicion of murder?

4.12 Review

The ten phrases in the box below all come from Unit 3. Write eight of them in the passage below. There will be two that you do not use at all.

scenic route
once-in-a-lifetime experience
sandy beaches long-haul plane journey
tourist trap crystal clear water
insect bites spectacular scenery
day-trippers padlock and chain

It is a cliché that we travel in order to remind ourselves of the benefits of home. Even when we read in the brochures that this resort has long ……… (1) or that island has ……… (2), we never really believe it. We already know that the ……… (3) we were promised in a travel agency in Bristol or Birmingham will turn out to be foamy, brownish detergent. We already know that the quiet, tranquil hilltop village will be a ……… (4) filled with ……… (5). We know that the bus which takes us on the ……… (6) from our hotel to the sea will be taking dangerous mountain bends at 80 kilometres per hour. And yet we still go. Even the discomfort (and cost) of a ……… (7), the waiting around at airports or coach stations, the prospect of ……… (8) as mosquitoes, flies and worse attack us in our beds or sleeping bags, none of these things stops us packing our bags and heading off for the sun. And all for that blessed sense of relief when we get back home.

You are what you eat

5.1 To start you thinking

a Write down everything that you ate or drank yesterday.

b Divide the list you made into two categories: foods which are good for you and foods which are bad for you.

5.2 Reading

You are going to read a newspaper article about a group of people whose diet has been found to be very healthy. Before you look at the text, answer the following questions.

a Which country do you think they live in? Do you think they live in the town or the countryside?

b Which of the following do you think will be mentioned in the diet?

cereals	beer	fish	meat
beans	milk	wine	fruit
whisky	chocolate	lentils	eggs
pasta	pizza	beans	cheese
salad	ice-cream	olive oil	vegetables

C Now read the article and check your answers to the questions in a and b.

Villagers' diet holds key to a healthy life

Liz Hunt   Health Editor

The simple diet followed by Greek villagers is the key to a long and healthy life and may protect against known health hazards such as smoking and lack of medical care, according to a study. 5

The Greek variant of the Mediterranean diet — which was first identified as beneficial to health more than 20 years ago — combines the best of current scientific knowledge on healthy eating. 10

But Dimitrios Tricholpoulos, from the Harvard School of Public Health, who analysed the diet of 182 Greek villagers aged 70 and over, says that it was the 'overall dietary pattern' which explained their longevity and general good health. 15

Their diet included whole-grain bread, potatoes and other cereals. 20

They ate cooked meals and soups, and salads rich in olive oil and accompanied by beans, lentils and vegetables in sizeable portions. Fresh fruit was a staple. 25

Milk intake was low but cheese and yoghurt was high. Feta cheese was added to salads and vegetable stews.

Meat was regarded as too expensive by most villagers, who preferred fish. 30

According to the report in the British Medical Journal, wine was consumed in moderation and almost always to accompany food. None of the pensioners was a heavy drinker: no man drank more than seven, and no woman more than two glasses of wine a day. 35

During the six-year study, 53 people died — 30 (57 per cent) of them men — and 17 (32 per cent) of them smokers. Of the 129 survivors, 61 (47 per cent) were men and 30 (23 per cent) were smokers. 40 45

Analysis of the individual diets showed that for those who ate more of the components of the traditional Greek diet, there was a 17 per cent reduction in mortality. 50

Their diet — low in saturated (animal) fats, high in monounsaturated fats, high in complex carbohydrates (from grains and legumes) and high in fibre (fruits and vegetables) — was naturally rich in protective antioxidant vitamins A, C, E, beta-carotene, important minerals and other chemicals, like polyphenols and anthocyanines, associated with good health. 55 60

This may explain the paradox that people living in rural areas of European Mediterranean countries smoke heavily and have poor access to medical care, but generally survive to a good age. 65

5.3 Grammar – relative pronouns

a Underline the relative pronouns/adverbs in the text below.

The Good Life

by Jemima Pugh-Smythe

A fanatical vegetarian <u>whom</u> I know was telling me about the virtues of the Greek diet. Greek villagers, whose lifestyle can be quite harsh, are said to live to a ripe old age despite a relative lack of health care. And the reason? Research suggests it's the food they eat that keeps them in good health. Their staple foods, which consist mainly of fresh fruit and vegetables, are known to be beneficial to anyone who eats them in sufficient quantities. What a surprising unforeseen advantage of living in a country where meat is too expensive – still, I don't think I'll be giving up the finer foods in life just yet!

b Write the relative pronouns/adverbs from the text and complete the table about when to use them.

Pronoun/adverb	Person	Thing	Place	Formal only
whom	✓	✗	✗	✓

c Look at the following sentences and decide which words from the box can go in the gaps. More than one may be possible.

who	which	that
whose	whom	x (no pronoun)

1 A good diet is one ...*which/that*... is enjoyable but healthy.

2 Meat was regarded as too expensive by most villagers, ... preferred fish.

3 The restaurant, ... was located on the waterfront, was dirty and crowded.

4 It was the kind of meal .... you enjoy because of the company.

5 The cookery course was very successful: about 250 people attended, of .... 247 passed the final exam.

6 It is a diet for slimmers .... don't want to give up eating.

7 The vegetables are grown in a completely natural environment, ... means they taste better.

8 Chef Marco Pierre White, ... new brasserie opens this week, is regarded as the enfant terrible of British cuisine.

5.4 Grammar – relative clauses

a The sentences below are all correct. Explain the differences in style and/or meaning.

1 a) The meat, which has been stored in the ship's fridge, was unsafe to eat.
   b) The meat which has been stored in the ship's fridge was unsafe to eat.

2 a) It's not a thing you should worry about.
   b) It's not a thing about which you should worry.

3 a) They cooked their meals on a 1930s gas fire, which surprised her mother.
   b) They cooked their meals on a 1930s gas fire, which used to belong to her mother.

4 a) He's a cookery writer I really like.
   b) He's a cookery writer that I really like.

5 a) Who did you make the reservation with?
   b) With whom did you make the reservation?

b Add the correct relative pronoun or adverb to the sentences below. Decide whether the sentences should contain defining or non-defining clauses, and add commas where necessary.

1 Chefs .... own restaurants have much more control over what is on the menu.

2 I brought some excellent wines back from Bordeaux .... is the first French city I've visited.

3 I hate peanuts .... is the reason I'm not fond of many Thai dishes.

4 I respect anyone .... knowledge of wines is as great as my own – though there aren't many around of course!

5 People .... smoke tend to have a much weaker sense of taste.

6 Simon Talbot .... sea-food restaurant has five stars in Gourmet's Guide is advertising a training course for new chefs.

7 The British beef industry .... had major exports in the early 1990s suffered badly from the effects of Mad Cow Disease before it was brought under control.

8 The English food at the barbecue was really boring, but I loved the food .... was from the Caribbean.

9 The factory .... my friend works makes most of the frozen food you see in supermarkets.

10 I've never eaten anything in my life .... has made me so ill.

5.5 To start you thinking

Which of the following sea-animals can you identify? Use a dictionary if necessary.

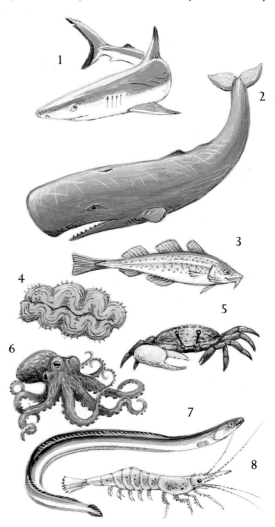

5.6 Reading

a Read the passage quickly and answer the following questions.

1 Which of the animals on the previous page are mentioned?

2 What do you think *chowder* is?

It was quite late in the evening when the little *Moss* came snugly to anchor, and Queequeg and I went ashore; so we could attend to no business that day, at least none but supper and a bed. The landlord of the Spouter-Inn had recommended
5 to us his cousin Hosea Hussey of the Twy Pots, whom he asserted to be the proprietor of one of the best kept hotels in Nantucket, and moreover he had assured us that Cousin Hosea, as he called him, was famous for his chowders.

        * * *

10   And so it turned out; Mr Hosea Hussey being from home, but leaving Mrs Hussey entirely competent to attend to all his affairs. Upon making known our desires for a supper and a bed, Mrs Hussey ... ushered us into a little room, and seating us at a table spread with the remains of a recently
15 concluded repast, turned round to us and said – 'Clam or Cod?'

     'What's that about Cods, ma'am?' said I with much politeness.

     'Clam or Cod?' she repeated.

20   'A clam for supper? a cold clam; is *that* what you mean, Mrs Hussey?' says I, 'but that's a rather cold and clammy reception in the winter time, ain't it, Mrs Hussey?'

     But being in a great hurry ... and seeming to hear nothing but the word 'clam', Mrs Hussey hurried towards an
25 open door leading to the kitchen, and bawling out 'clam for two', disappeared.

     'Queequeg,' said I, 'do you think that we can make a supper for us both on one clam?'

     However, a warm savoury steam from the kitchen
30 served to belie the apparently cheerless prospect before us. But when that smoking chowder came in, the mystery was delightfully explained. Oh, sweet friends! hearken to me. It was made of small juicy clams, scarcely bigger than hazel nuts, mixed with pounded ship biscuit, and salted pork cut up
35 into little flakes; the whole enriched with butter, and plentifully seasoned with pepper and salt. Our appetites being sharpened by the frosty voyage, and in particular, Queequeg seeing his favourite fishy food before him, and the chowder being surpassingly excellent, we despatched it with great
40 expedition; when leaning back a moment and bethinking me of Mrs Hussey's calm cool announcement, I thought I would

try a little experiment. Stepping to the kitchen door, I uttered the word 'cod' with great emphasis, and resumed my seat. In a few moments the savoury steam came forth again, but with a different flavour, and in good time a fine cod-chowder was 45 placed before us.

     We resumed business, and while plying our spoons in the bowl, thinks I to myself, I wonder now if this has any effect on the head? What's that stultifying saying about chowder-headed people? 'But look, Queequeg, ain't that a live 50 eel in your bowl? Where's your harpoon?'

     Fishiest of all fishy places was the Twy Pots, which well deserved its name; for the pots there were always boiling chowders. Chowder for breakfast, and chowder for dinner, and chowder for supper, until you began to look for fishbones 55 coming through your clothes. The area before the house was paved with clam-shells. Mrs Hussey wore a polished necklace of cod vertebrae; and Hosea Hussey had his accounts-books bound in superior old shark-skin. There was a fishy flavour to the milk, too, which I could not at all account for, until one 60 morning happening to take a stroll along the beach among some fishermen's boats, I saw Hosea's brindled cow feeding on fish remnants, and marching along the sand with each foot in a cod's decapitated head, looking very slipshod, I assure ye. 65

     Supper concluded, we received a lamp, and directions from Mrs Hussey concerning the nearest way to bed; but, as Queequeg was about to precede me up the stairs, the lady stretched forth her arms and demanded his harpoon; she allowed no harpoon in her chambers. 'Why not?' said I, 'every 70 true whaleman sleeps with his harpoon – but why not!' 'Because it's dangerous,' says she. 'Ever since young Stiggs coming from that unfortunate v'y'ge of his when he was gone four years and a half, with only three barrels of *ile*, was found dead in my first floor back, with his harpoon in his side; ever 75 since then I allow no boarders to take sich dangerous weapons in their rooms a-night. So, Mr Queequeg' (for she had learned his name), 'I will just take this here iron, and keep it for you till morning. But the chowder; clam or cod to-morrow for breakfast, men?' 80

     'Both,' says I, 'and let's have a couple of smoked herring by way of variety.'

b **Read the text again more carefully and answer the following questions.**

1 What kind of book does this text come from?

2 Do you think the text was written in modern times? Why (not)?

3 Which of the following adjectives would suitably describe the text?

tragic ironic amusing exciting horrific poetic

4 Where and how do you think the writer ('I') and Queequeg are travelling?

5 Can you speculate what happens before and after this passage?

6 In your opinion, what is the relationship between Queequeg and the writer?

7 What seems to be their job or occupation?

8 Have they been to this hotel before? How do we know?

9 Which of the following adjectives would you use to describe Mrs Hussey?

abrupt loud friendly strict romantic cheerful sentimental polite absent-minded

10 What is the misunderstanding in lines 19-22?

11 The Twy Pots is described as a 'fishy place' (line 52). What evidence does the writer produce to show this?

12 Why did Mrs Hussey not allow harpoons in her chambers?

13 When Mrs Hussey says 'this here iron' in line 78, what is she talking about?

C **Find words or phrases in the text which mean the following:**

1 a small sea-animal in a shell that can be eaten

2 listen

3 thick fish or sea-food soup

4 a meal

5 closely and comfortably

6 on to the shore

7 shout in a loud, rough voice

8 to show someone the way

5.7 Vocabulary

a List all the names of food mentioned in the passage.

b The following brain map is about food. Some words have already been filled in. Add at least five words from the passage, and as many words as you can from your own word-store.

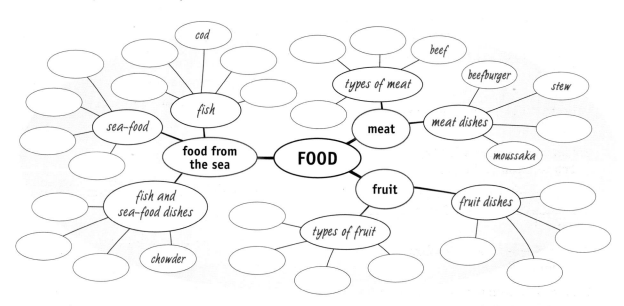

5.8 Idioms from food and eating

a Look at the following idioms and sayings, which are all based around the topic of food or eating:

1 for all the tea in China
2 packed like sardines
3 as nutty as a fruitcake
4 to make a pig of yourself
5 a big cheese
6 the best thing since sliced bread
7 no ...worth their salt
8 on the breadline
9 to save someone's bacon
10 food for thought

Listen to the ten dialogues, and, working in pairs or small groups, decide from the context what the idioms mean.

b For each idiom, decide what you would say in your own language.

5.9 Hearing perception

Follow the instructions given by your teacher.

5.10 Pronunciation – contrastive stress

a Listen to the following words, phrases and numbers, and mark where the main stress comes, by drawing a bubble over the stressed word, or part of the word.

Example: *He used to live in London.*

1 He used to live in London.
2 fish pie
3 go on a diet
4 245 milligrams
5 It was made from beef and potatoes.
6 You have to boil it for about ten minutes.
7 672294
8 John MacDonald

57

b Now listen to the same phrases in two-line dialogues. Mark where the main stress is now. Is it in the same place? Why not?

1 He's worked in London, hasn't he?
   No, he used to live in London, but he's never worked there.

2 You're going to have the cottage pie, then?
   No, I'm going to have the fish pie. John's having the cottage pie.

3 I'm surprised Fiona's given up her diet.
   No, I said she's decided to go on a diet.

4 Peter said the result was 345 milligrams.
   245 milligrams, you mean …

5 And it's made from beef and potatoes, is it?
   No, it was made from beef and potatoes, but that was before the beef scare!

6 So you fry it for ten minutes …
   No, you have to boil it for about ten minutes.

7 Is your fax number 642294?
   672294.

8 Did you say John O'Donald?
   John MacDonald.

c Now practise the dialogues in pairs.

d Work in pairs. One of you is a rather stupid chef about to go on television to show the viewers how to make a cake. Your instructions are in the recipe above. The other student is the chef's personal assistant. The chef goes through the instructions, making lots of mistakes. The assistant corrects the chef, **using only stress to make the correction.**

Example:

CHEF: *So you put the cake in the fridge for thirty minutes …*

ASSISTANT: *No, you put the cake in the* **oven** *for thirty minutes …*

Speedy Sponge Cake

INGREDIENTS:

2 large eggs
100 grams of flour
125 grams of sugar
125 grams of butter
a spoonful of cocoa

INSTRUCTIONS:

1 Put all the ingredients in a large bowl, and mix with a wooden spoon.
2 If the mixture is very thick, add a few drops of warm water.
3 Grease a circular 18cm baking tray.
4 Put the mixture in the tray.
5 Heat the oven to 170 degrees C.
6 Cook in the middle of the oven for thirty minutes.
7 Remove from the cooking tray immediately, and leave to cool.
8 Sprinkle some icing sugar on top.

(5.11) **Review**

Write one word from Unit 4 in each space.

When the policewoman asked the man to go to the police station with her, he *...threatened.....* (1) to hit her. Although the man was angry and upset, the police finally managed to take him into .... (2). He was allowed to leave the police station on .... (3). Like many other criminals, his case never came to court because of a lack of .... (4). This was surprising, since the police had caught him .... (5). Also, they had found several pieces of stolen .... (6) in his flat. Some of these had been stolen in a ram-........... (7) which had taken place in the city centre in March. Although he was asked more than six times, the man .... (8) to say where he had got the stolen objects.

Money makes the world go round

6.1 To start you thinking

Working in pairs or groups, discuss the meanings of the following common sayings to do with money. Also decide whether each one shows money to be a good thing, a bad thing or neither.

1 Money talks.

2 The love of money is the root of all evil. (The Bible)

3 A fool and his money are soon parted.

4 Every man has his price.

5 It's money for old rope.

6 Look after the pennies and the pounds will look after themselves.

7 Neither a borrower nor a lender be. (Shakespeare)

8 Money can't buy you love. (The Beatles)

9 It's the rich that get the pleasure. It's the poor that get the blame.

10 Money doesn't grow on trees.

6.2 Reading

a Look at the six statements on the right, then read the article below. Put a tick (✔) after the statements which agree with ideas expressed in the article and a cross (✗) after those which do not.

THE NATIONAL LOTTERY®

Maybe, just maybe.™

1 The poorest areas of Britain receive most grants from the National Lottery.

2 People from richer areas spend more on the lottery than those from poorer areas.

3 In the USA, 25 states use lotteries as a way of financing public spending.

4 The statistics from Chicago show that some poor people spend about 20 times more on lottery tickets than better-off people.

5 The article shows that poor Americans spend more on lotteries than poor Britons.

6 One conclusion is that lotteries are a type of tax on the poor but not on the rich.

PENNIES FROM HEAVEN

RESEARCH disclosed last week in the *National Lottery Yearbook* (which is not, by the way, published by Camelot but by an independent body called the Directory of Social Change) showed that the common suspicion was correct: it's the rich wot get the gravy, especially if they live in south-east England. The study showed interesting disparities in the distribution of the £1.4bn which has so far been given to 'good causes', including in that category (which I'm certain it is, from his wife's point of view) the funding of Winston Churchill Jr's divorce. By the end of last year some of the poorest local authority districts in Britain – Newham, Barking, South Tyneside – had received grants from Lottery funds which worked out, per head of their populations, at £1.10, 90p and £1.78. Meanwhile, the three richest local authority districts – Mid-Sussex, Aylesbury Vale and East Hertford – received £9.02, £9.24 and £16.08. The 5 per cent of England's population who live in its most deprived areas got much less than half their fair share of the grants.

We have, then, some detailed ideas of who receives what. But might it not also be fundamental to our understanding of the Lottery's fairness to identify by social class and area the people who raise the revenue? The money, contrary to the implications of the advertising, doesn't drop from heaven.

The punter pays, and I suspect that there are proportionately more punters in Newham, Barking and South Tyneside than in Mid-Sussex, Aylesbury Vale and East Hertford.

That is certainly the American experience. Lotteries started to grow as an instrument of public finance in the United States about 25 years ago. Today 39 states have them and use them to fund social programmes such as education. In 1994, for example, Illinois spent more than $500m from lottery funds on schools. Where does the money come from? Here are some figures taken from an excellent Chicago magazine called *The Baffler*. In Flossmoor, an affluent Chicago suburb where the average household income is $117,000 a year, households spent an average of $4.48 in lottery tickets. In Posen, a poor suburb where the average household income is $53,000, the monthly average is $91.82.

As Kim Phillips writes in *The Baffler*, the Illinois Lottery allows the state to raise money almost solely from 'poor and working people'. Also: 'While the Lottery may, in a sense, be rational for the individual, it is clearly irrational for the class … The poor donate money to make one of their number rich, at which point that person and their new-found wealth pack up and move out. And the rich pay nothing for this self-containing system of political quiescence – in fact, they get a tax cut.'

b 'Reading between the lines' is understanding something which is not expressed overtly or directly by the writer. Look back at the article and answer the following questions.

1 What do you think 'Camelot' does?

2 What does the writer mean by 'gravy'?

3 Which of the sayings in 6.1 is 'get the gravy' based on?

4 Why does the writer put 'good causes' between inverted commas?

5 What is the writer's opinion of Winston Churchill Jnr?

6 What do you think 'the implications of the advertising' are?

7 What do you think a 'punter' does?

8 Why is it possible to see lotteries as 'rational for the individual' but 'irrational for the class'?

6.3 Discussion

In small groups, discuss your answers to the following questions.

1 Are principles always more important than money?

2 Have you (or has anyone you know) ever done anything you (or they) regret for money?

3 What is your attitude to money? Is money wholly bad, wholly good or do you have mixed feelings?

6.4 Reading

a You are going to read a passage entitled *Freedom, money and morality*. Write down five adjectives, five nouns and five verbs which you predict will appear in the text. When you have finished, compare your predictions in groups and explain your choices.

b Now read the text and check your predictions.

Freedom, money and *morality*

Dorothy Rowe

If there is one universal rule, it is 'in making money you can break the law and get away with it, provided the sums of money involved are huge'. Steal a few hundred dollars and you will go to jail. Steal a hundred million and the worst that can happen to you 5 is that you will have to live in luxury in some foreign clime.

This is not just because if you are rich, you can afford good lawyers. Dishonesty on a massive scale involves many people, most of whom like to think of themselves as honest and upright. They will use their power and influence to 10 protect themselves, and thus you.

Why do people stray from their principles when money is in the offing? **A** There is also our fundamental insecurity – of being always in danger of being overwhelmed by events in a world over which we 15 have so little control. With money we can demand that the world be what we want it to be. So one famous banker, who in 1990 faced a bankruptcy petition for millions of pounds and a long set of criminal charges, suns himself in northern Cyprus, and Mrs Jones is banged up in Holloway because 20 she cannot pay her television licence. ⟶

61

The callousness of the market and the fine distinctions we all make about the importance of money was something I learnt about early in life. My mother disapproved of gambling. She discovered that my father had given his 25 brother money to help him with a gambling debt and threatened to end their marriage.

Mother had a habit of hiding special things in the oven. One evening dad arrived home and found her in tears. Because the weather had suddenly turned cold, she had lit the stove 30 and burnt a very special pair of silk stockings. Dad reached into his pocket, took out a wad of notes and offered them to her. They could have come from only one place, a bookmaker's. **B** [   ]

C [   ] In my mother's case, I know 35 why. She was the fourth of six in a family where blows and harsh words were plenty and kisses rare, and so the hole inside her was as wide and deep as the Pacific.

The fact that we go around with these holes inside us is not an excuse for being greedy or behaving dishonestly. 40 **D** [   ]

We need to consider as well our responsibility to other people and the consequences of our actions.

If it is wrong to steal a million from a company, is it also wrong to steal small quantities of that company's 45 stationery? A personnel manager told me how she had done some research on the quantity of stationery lost when employees think along the lines of 'I need a new hole punch at home, so I'll take this one and order another through stationery'. The total value of the stuff taken made it a major 50 crime. Such activity can arise from having a relativist view with very relaxed definitions of right and wrong, or an absolutist view and be well practised in fudging.

By fudging I mean big leaps in argument, changing the meanings of the words used from one statement to another 55 and ignoring the inconvenient facts to arrive at a conclusion that benefits the fudger.

Understanding our lack of virtue is simply a matter of observing what happens to us and how we interpret what happens to us. **E** [   ] 60

We are all born lacking a conscience, not because we are inherently wicked, but because we lack the concepts necessary for a conscience. Once we discover other people and have the chance to form a bond with one mothering person, we soon acquire a conscience, because we realise 65 that to maintain this bond, we have sometimes to relinquish our own needs and wishes and defer to someone else. We can no longer be totally selfish, though sometimes we might try.

C **Now choose the best sentence to fill each of the blanks (A–E) in the article. Be careful, one of the suggested answers does not fit at all.**

1 Because money means more – more choice, more freedom, more goodies.

2 It is simply one of the factors we need to take into account when we are choosing how we live our lives.

3 Why does the chance of getting money so often override our most dearly held principles?

4 The truth of the matter is that no money equals no power equals no enjoyment.

5 Morality is concerned with how we behave towards one another.

6 Without a word she reached out and took the money.

6.5 Discourse

What do the words in **bold** from the article refer to?

1 **This** is not just because if you are rich, … (line 7)

2 most of **whom** like to think of themselves … (line 9)

3 over **which** we have so little control … (line 15)

4 suns **himself** in northern Cyprus … (line 19)

5 money to help **him** with a gambling debt … (line 26)

6 threatened to end **their** marriage. … (line 27)

7 **They** could have come from only one place … (line 33)

8 **where** blows and harsh words were plenty … (line 36)

9 and order **another** through stationery … (line 49)

10 **Such** activity can arise … (line 51)

6.6 Writing – giving examples

When expressing an opinion or arguing a case in written English, it is better if you can add examples. In many cases, the examples add interest too.

The way you introduce examples after the generalised idea or sentiment can be by using **brackets**:

Pacific Ring countries (**Korea, Vietnam, Cambodia**) have made tremendous economic progress over the last few decades.

or by using **fixed expressions**:

Some British pop musicians **such as** Paul McCartney, Elton John or the Gallagher brothers have become mega-rich.

The public are constantly encouraged to eat food rich in fibre **e.g.** fruit, vegetables and brown bread.

Look at the expressions in the box below, which are all used to present an example or examples. Using an English-English dictionary, find out how they are used and how formal, neutral or informal they are. Then complete the sentences that follow in an appropriate way. (Don't forget you can use brackets too!)

> like   such as   for example
> for instance   and suchlike
> take for instance   e.g.
> examples abound/include
> exemplified by   from … to …
> an/one obvious example is
> spring to mind   number amongst them
> including   to name/mention but a few

1 Over the past few years, we have experienced numerous economic problems in my country, …

2 It is very common for a person who has 'made it' in one way or another to go into personal decline. …

3 Many companies offer attractive fringe benefits or 'perks' to their employees …

4 There are many ways of paying for things as well as good old cash. …

5 Thousands of people, including youngsters, are now addicted to some form of gambling …

6 If you wish to invest your money ethically, there are various options available to you. …

7 There are quite a lot of shops round here that offer discounts to students on all sorts of things …

8 Governments never seem to lack imagination when it comes to identifying things they can tax. …

9 Customers often complain about the poor service they get from their bank …

10 Spending half an hour a week organising your finances could actually save you thousands of pounds over a lifetime. There are so many 'little' things that we miss; …

11 There are only a few 'hard' convertible currencies in the world …

63

12 Our highly experienced advisers can help you with all aspects of handling your finances, …

6.7 Grammar – *ing* forms

a Look at the examples and complete the descriptions of the uses of ~ing forms.

1 Ralph's always *enjoyed getting* something for nothing.
It's not worth breaking the law.
Certain ……… and ……… are always followed by an ~ing form.

2 I couldn't care less *about doing* what's right!
You should think twice *before telling* a lie.
A verb after a ……… is always an ~ing form.

3 They try to tell us that *banking* is an honest business!
Drinking tends to make people less able to act responsibly, I find.
Some ~ing forms can be used as true ……… in some contexts.

4 *Making* more money is all entrepreneurs care about.
Sheila always gives something to beggars despite *having little herself.*
An ~ing form can be used to make a noun ……… .

5 *People earning a lot of money* should pay a lot of tax.
The president made a public apology, *making it easier for the electorate to forgive him.*
Some reduced ……… clauses use an ~ing form.

b Match the examples below with the explanations in part a.

a A hedonist is a person who believes that having fun is the only purpose in life. ………

b Advertising seeks to persuade rather than inform. ………

c I've thought of investing in the stock market, but as a socialist I don't really approve of it. ………

d It's no use blaming other people; you have to take responsibility for the situation you're in and do something about it yourself! ………

e Western multinational companies marketing their goods in the developing world are often less scrupulous in their methods. ………

c Now look at these examples of the uses of ~ing forms from the passage in 6.4. and explain the use of ~ing forms.

1 My mother disapproved of gambling.

2 Mother had a habit of hiding special things in the oven.

3 Understanding our lack of virtue is simply a matter of …

d Some of the sentences below need ~ing forms and some don't. Complete them using the correct form of the verb.

1 Come on, there's work .... (do). Time is money, remember!

2 Have you considered .... (tell) the police about these blackmail threats?

3 It's no use .... (dream) of what you can't have.

4 Many self-employed are forced .... (sell) their houses if their companies go bankrupt.

5 Most people just want .... (earn) enough to lead an easy life.

6 Politicians are only anxious .... (please) as many voters as possible.

7 Rumour has it that she got to the top by .... (cheat) her former business partners.

8 There's psychological research .... (show) that the rich tend to be happier than the poor.

9 When the jackpot number was announced, she didn't know whether .... (laugh) or cry.

10 .... (win) the lottery still seems to be the answer to everyone's prayer.

6.8 Listening

Before you listen, answer these quiz questions in pairs.

1 Which country has a stock exchange index called the 'Footsie'?

2 Is the Australian currency the dollar or the pound?

3 What's the interest rate in the country you're in now?

4 What's the name of the US stock exchange?

5 If a company is about to be 'taken over', do its shares usually increase or decrease in value?

 Now look at the graphs and notes and listen to the radio extract. Then complete the graphs, the table and the notes.

a

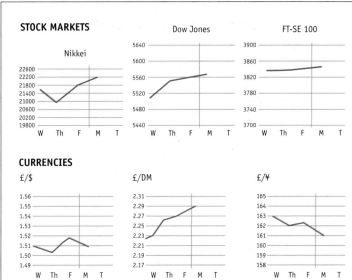

b

YOUR HOLIDAY POUND	
Australia	.... **dollars**
Canada	**2.04 dollars**
France	.... **francs**
Germany	.... **marks**
Italy	.... **lire**
Portugal	**220 escudos**
Spain	.... **pesetas**
Turkey	**75,000 lire**
United States	**1.54 dollars**

c

LATEST NEWS!

_____ Bank planning to _____
over Middlehampton _____ _____ .
Middlehampton share price up by about £ _____ —
from _____ p to _____ p!

_____ building company made 6-monthly profit
of (only) £ _____ — shares _____ from
_____ p to _____ p!

Pronunciation
– silent letters

English spelling is often very little help with pronunciation. Silent letters, for example, make pronunciation difficult. Some words are 'one-offs', e.g. mortgage / mɔːgɪdʒ /. Many, however, fall into groups with fixed combinations of silent letters, e.g. **kn**ow / nəʊ /, dou**bt** / daʊt /, **wr**itten / rɪtən /.

a Working in pairs, find the silent letters in the words below and organise them into groups. Some may be in two groups! Here are some combinations to get you started:

wr... kn... ...mb

wrestling	bomb	solemn	column
salmon	knee	listen	answer
plumber	guarantee	autumn	scene
climb	wrinkles	knock	castle
island	guest	knight	receipt
debt	science	guide	wrist
scissors	muscle	palm	design
sword	fasten		

Remember to add to your lists as you come across new words with silent letters.

 b Cross out the silent letters in these sentences. Then listen to the tape and practise saying them.

1 Everyone condemned the rise in interest rates.

2 The building society repossessed the house as they couldn't pay the mortgage.

3 We were disappointed not to get a Christmas bonus.

4 Hugh couldn't stand the hustle and bustle of working in the Stock Exchange.

5 Bad debts completely wrecked their business.

6 Banking in the Cayman Islands might be the answer to your tax problems.

7 The bank manager was doubtful whether the scheme would work.

8 Jack was given an expensive wristwatch to soften the blow of being made redundant.

9 The plumber didn't give me a receipt and couldn't even guarantee it wouldn't break down again.

10 The manager resigned after the advertising campaign failed to attract any foreign investors.

 ## 6.10 Review

One of the three words in italics comes from Unit 5 and is correct in context. Choose the correct word.

1 They *bowled/bawled/balled* at us angrily to sit down.

2 When the fire's burning, it's nice and *snug/snuck/snack* in here on a winter's evening.

3 *Jam/Lamb/Clam* chowder is a type of soup, very popular in New England.

4 We're so poor we're practically on the bread *slice/line/board*.

5 It looked like a sea snake but it was just an *eel/ear/ale*.

6 Judith's rather shocking description of everyday life in India really gave us *fruit/food/fuel* for thought.

7 We collected some *crumbs/crops/crabs* in a bucket while walking along the beach.

8 Any cook worth his *salt/pepper/sugar* should be able to produce a good soufflé.

9 It was the only train to the beach and we were packed inside like *sausages/cigarettes/sardines*.

10 We didn't think we'd have enough money but then Joe offered to lend us £500 – he really saved our *pork/ham/bacon*.

Back to nature

7.1 To start you thinking

a Match the words in A with their partners in B. Use a good English–English dictionary to help you.

A

> tree- big national wildlife whale rain eco-conscious rubber- natural dugout nesting nature

B

> tapper conservation politicians birds game canoe park felling watching history safari forests

b In pairs or groups, discuss how these things are connected with nature and the environment.

67

7.2 Reading

a Read this short introductory paragraph to a magazine interview and answer the questions. Identify the words in the paragraph that help you.

> **Tony Samphier talks to the woman who has emerged from a new generation of eco-conscious politicians in Brazil to be dubbed an 'Amazon legend'.**

1 What is this woman's job?

2 Do we know how old she is?

3 What's her nationality?

4 What do you think she's trying to do?

5 Has she been successful?

b Now read the interview slowly and carefully. Check your answers to part a and answer the following questions.

1 Why does Marina want to save the Amazonian rain forest?

2 In what way did hepatitis benefit Marina?

3 What important lesson about leadership did Marina learn from Chico Mendes?

4 What does Marina see as the function of the Green Party?

5 Have Marina's political views changed over the years?

c In your notebook, explain the significance to Marina of the following.

1 Acre

2 farofa de paca

3 three (2 possible answers)

4 fifteen years old

5 Chico Mendes

6 PT

7 1988

8 empates

9 Gandhi

10 slash-and-burn developers

MARINA

'When I fly over the Amazon by plane I love to look at the green carpet of forest, criss-crossed by rivers,' says Marina Silva, who took her seat in the Brazilian Senate last January after an unexpected election win in the Amazon state of Acre. The national daily *Jornal do Brasil* described it as a 'victory of the dream over circumstance'. 5

'I feel a great sense of pain when I see an area of deforestation,' she says. 'I fear Amazonia will end up with the same devastation as in Europe and the United States if we don't stop what's happening.' But she is not interested in saving the forest for its own sake alone. From an early age, she learned its value: people depend on it for food, work and pleasure. So her prescription relies as much on the sustainable use of its resources as on conservation. 10 15

A reference to her favourite meal underlines the point: 'I hope the ecologists will forgive me,' she says, 'but in the rubber-tapper settlement where I lived as a child, game was very important. I still haven't forgotten the taste of a good *farofa de paca* (a large forest rodent, roasted with cassava).' 20

Silva's rise to prominence stems from a struggle for life itself. 'My mother had eleven children, but three died. I was the eldest of the survivors and so I helped to look after the others.' 25

There was no school where the family lived. Silva worked extracting rubber until she was sixteen, often going without food for up to 24 hours. She was still illiterate at fourteen. A year later her mother died. 'I had to acquire a little knowledge to help my father calculate the weight of the rubber,' she explains. 30

The experience whetted Silva's appetite for education. Then, at sixteen, she contracted hepatitis. Ironically this helped her to realise her dream. No longer able to do the heavy rubber-tapping work, she moved to the city to study. In just three years she completed and passed all the necessary exams to enter university. 35 40

When rubber-tappers' union president Chico Mendes helped found the Workers Party (PT) and decided to be an election candidate in Acre, she joined him.

SILVA

45 They worked together in the trade union movement and set up a congress in Acre. His assassination in 1988 was a personal tragedy for her.

50 'We had many years of companionship which cannot be easily summarised, but if I hadn't known him, my life would have been much the poorer for it,' says Silva. 'What I have clearest in 55 my mind is Chico himself, his way of being, his style of leadership. He knew how to listen and let everyone else speak, and only later would he make up his own mind. This 60 is a very important lesson he left me.'

For both of them the biggest test came with the *empates*, the human-barrier campaigns against the tree-felling which saved thousands of hectares of forest.

Though trade unionists and environmentalists are often 65 the targets of intimidation and violence, non-violence is an important part of Silva's political armour: 'I have a great admiration for people who struggle in the way Gandhi did: at once activist and pacifist.' As a local councillor in Rio Branco, the capital of Acre, she had to 70 fight tooth and nail to get local conservatives to declare an official day of remembrance for Mendes. In the end she won.

Her current political success reflects the way environmental and social activists of her generation in 75 Brazil have chosen to fight within the PT rather than the small Green Party. In their view the Greens deal with parks and flowers while the PT grapples with the socio-environmental crisis.

'I identify with people who want a party of proposals, of 80 dialogue with other parties and with civil society,' says Silva – a coded message that she has moved away from the far-left politics of her youth. 'The PT was the logical option,' she concludes.

Today, already described as an 'Amazon legend' by the 85 Brazilian press, Silva is a force to be reckoned with in the battle for the life and soul of the Amazon – the slash-and-burn developers and the big landowners versus those who need the forest for their survival.

7.3) Collocations

a Find the collocations used in the passage to replace the words in brackets.

1 .... (stimulated) her appetite

2 .... (caught) hepatitis

3 .... (make come true) her dream

4 .... (start) a political party

5 .... (struggle) with a crisis

6 fight .... (very hard)

7 green .... (covering) of forest

8 someone's rise to ....
(importance and fame)

9 .... (called/known as) a legend

10 .... (feel) hunger

b Now use the collocations (there are two extra) to complete the following sentences.

1 John's prepared to .... to stop them building a motorway through the wood.

2 The Green Party first .... in Britain in the early 60s.

3 The Environment Minister's job is to .... with the never-ending problems caused by unthinking capitalists.

4 That trip to the zoo really .... Tim's .... for studying wildlife. He's going on safari next week.

5 Thousands of rabbits .... myxomatosis so the population has been decimated in this area.

6 Suzy .... her dream when she was offered the post of head of marine biology.

7 Jonathon Porritt, who helped to .... Friends of the Earth, is now a writer and broadcaster.

8 Britain has been .... 'the dirty man of Europe' for its part in contributing to the acid rain problem in Scandinavia.

7.4) Grammar – conditional sentences

a Look at these conditional sentences from the reading passage in 7.2, then underline and label the condition and result in the three sentences below.

I fear _Amazonia will end up with the same devastation ..._   if _we don't stop what's happening._
result   **condition**

... if _I hadn't known him,_   _my life would have been much the poorer._
condition   **result**

1 The article suggests that if Marina Silva hadn't got hepatitis, she might not have become a student.

2 The likelihood is that she wouldn't have been able to help Chico Mendes set up a Workers Party Congress if she hadn't gained an education.

3 If she hadn't become involved in politics, it's doubtful that she'd be the 'Amazon legend' she is today.

b It is important to understand clearly the tenses used in conditionals because they change the meaning. Match the conditionals with their descriptions of use, and say what grammar is used.

Type	Examples	Description
ZERO ....*b*....	If multinational companies take control of a region, the local people always suffer. If photosynthesis is taking place, oxygen is released into the atmosphere.	a Used for a highly improbable, hypothetical or imaginary condition in the present or future and its result. CONDITION: RESULT:
FIRST	If an asteroid hits the earth, it will be the end of civilisation. If I haven't heard from you in two days, I'm going to send help to find you.	b Used for general truths, such as scientific laws, which are always true in general time. CONDITION: *present tense/aspect* RESULT: *present tense/aspect*
SECOND	If people weren't so selfish, the world might be a happier place. If you were thinking of joining a pressure group, which one would it be?	c Used for conditions and results which don't fit into the time patterns of typical conditionals. Most usually, but not always, they describe a condition in the past and a result in the present. CONDITION: RESULT:
THIRD	If the dinosaurs hadn't been wiped out, I doubt the human race could have evolved very far at all. If the safari guide had been paying attention instead of chatting up the tourists, the lion would never have got him!	d Used for a possible condition in the future, and its future result. CONDITION: RESULT:
MIXED	If those bushmen hadn't found me, I mightn't be sitting here telling you this story. If governments had been doing their job properly, there wouldn't be a hole in the ozone layer!	e Used for a condition in the past that did not exist/occur, and its result, which also never happened. CONDITION: RESULT:

c Rephrase the ideas below as conditional sentences.

1 I hope it won't rain on Sunday, then we can go bird watching.

2 The wolf attacked only because you frightened it.

3 I can't tell you what type of snake it is because I don't know.

4 Joe wants to be a vet but he must pass his exams first.

5 We're not in hospital because we didn't touch that strange plant in the jungle.

6 Mating a zebra with a donkey results in a 'zedonk'!

7 They didn't see the rhino in time and crashed into it.

8 I remembered to bring the map, that's why we're not lost!

9 Swimming with crocodiles usually leads to death!

10 Sally doesn't speak very good Portuguese so she's not going to apply for that conservation job in Brazil.

(7.5) Reading

a Read the following questions, then scan through advertisements A–G to answer the questions.

1 For which advertisement do you need to send a large envelope?

2 How much does the mini TV camera cost?

3 Who should you contact if you're interested in Operation Wallacea?

4 Where could you see a jaguar?

5 What type of holiday is Eco Traveller advertising?

6 Could Cameras Underwater help you with a fault in your camera?

7 What is the shortest period a green volunteer could work for?

8 Does Subbuteo sell anything except books?

9 Where might you be able to photograph ring-tail lemurs?

10 What type of expert is Chris Majors?

A

ECOTRAVELLER
NATURAL HISTORY
WAKE UP TO THE NEW AGE OF ENVIRONMENTALLY RESPONSIBLE TOURISM
People, Culture, Wildlife and the Environment
Telephone: 01268 752 827
Fax: 01268 759 834
E-mail: tourdesk@aol.com
EXPEDITIONS

B

The "Medivet Minder 2"
Miniature Video T.V. Camera with Auto Focus Infrared and Sound

Watch!

NESTING BIRDS AND WILD ANIMALS IN THE DARK!

The "Medivet Minder Mark 2" Surveillance Camera connects into your own Domestic TV or VCR. This Miniature Camera, with Sound, also incorporates infrared light so can be used in nesting boxes or close to night time feeding areas for animals.
JUST SIT BACK AND WATCH IT ALL ON YOUR OWN TV!

Also ideal for close-ups on your bird table.
Can be used as a security camera through your VCR.
ONLY £299
Price includes 50m cable, P&P and VAT
Order now from:
MEDIVET LTD. 60 TOWER STREET, HARROGATE
N. YORKSHIRE HG1 IHS
Credit Cards/Cheques: Tel: 01423 509411 (24 hours)

C

OPERATION WALLACEA

Marine Expeditions based on our 'live-aboard'

- Scientific/photographic surveys of the reefs of Tukangbesi in Sulawesi, Indonesia, will continue for another year to help with the management plans of the newly created National Park.

- Expedition cruises to Marine National Parks and protected areas of Bali, Lombok, Komodo, Flores and Alor are also being run with opportunities to see the giant Komodo Dragon and go whale watching.

- Daily lectures, informal instruction, and dive tuition all included in the price.

Wildlife and Cultural Expeditions

- Explore the forest and reefs of Sulawesi with our resident scientists and dive instructors, plus a rare opportunity to learn about the Bajo people's unique sea-dwelling lifestyle with anthropologist Chris Majors.

- Explore the forest and Mayan ruins on Honduras and Guatemala with scientists and Mayan Shaman Dr Eric Estrada. Finish with a few days in Belize snorkelling with "friendly" sharks and dancing with rays!!

For further details contact Eileen or Helen

at Operation Wallacea

Tel: +44 (0) 1790 763665 Fax: +44 (0) 1790 763417

alternatively e-mail: tcoles@ecosurveys.win-uk.net

D

Don't take risks with the elements

Protective covers and watertight housings for SLR, Video and compact cameras, radio pouches, map safes, etc.

UNDERWATER PHOTOGRAPHY
Sales & Servicing

Cameras Underwater

East Island Farmhouses, Slade Road, Ottery St Mary, Devon, EX11 1OM
Telephone 01494 812277   Fax: 01494 8122274

E

GREEN VOLUNTEERS

The World Guide to Voluntary Work in Nature Conservation

More than 100 projects to work from one week to one year, for £10.00 (+ post)

For info send 11 x 22 cm SAE to:
BOX 360, 56 Gloucester Road
Kensington, London SW7 4UB
or call: 01767 262481

F

EXPLORE
small group exploratory holidays
SAFARIS WORLDWIDE

With Explore you could encounter big game in Kenya or Tanzania, go whale-watching in Newfoundland, see jaguar in the rain forests of Costa Rica. You could join a tiger safari in India, photograph ring-tail lemurs in Madagascar, spot rare birds in Brazil's Pantanal, paddle a dugout canoe through Botswana's Okavango Delta . . . PLUS Zimbabwe, Namibia, Nepal, Borneo, Galapagos, Assam . . .

Call us now for superb colour brochure!

Explore Worldwide (BW), Aldershot, GU11 1LQ
Tel: 01252 344161 (24 hrs)

G

SUBBUTEO
NATURAL HISTORY BOOKS LTD

The dependable, experienced, worldwide mail order book service. Specialists in all aspects of the natural sciences, wildlife and birdlife, plus travel books and maps. Including all books in print featured in BBC Wildlife.

FREE CATALOGUE on REQUEST

TEL: +44 (0)1352 736331
FAX: +44 (0)1352 736004

PISTYLL FARM, NERCYWYS
Nr WOLD, FLINTSHIRE
CH7 4EW, UK

b Decide which of the following sections of the classified advertisements each advertisement is taken from. There is one extra section.

Conservation   Books   Pets and wildlife
Worldwide   Societies   Photography

c Which of the advertisements above interests you most? Discuss your preferences in small groups.

7.6) Writing – leaflet

A good leaflet has an obvious focus and message. It is immediately clear, concise and eye-catching, often with a bold title and picture. Look at this simple example.

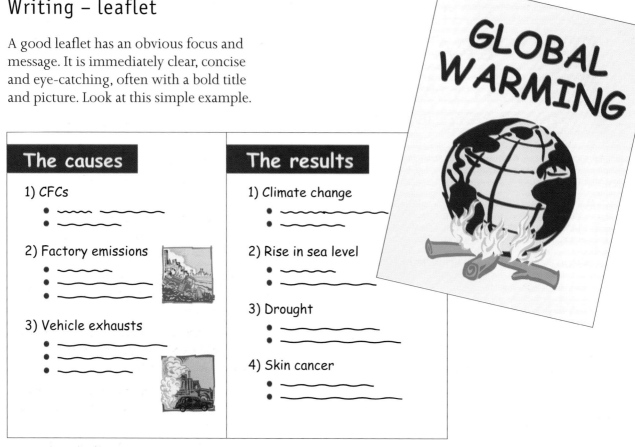

The causes	**The results**
1) CFCs	1) Climate change
2) Factory emissions	2) Rise in sea level
3) Vehicle exhausts	3) Drought
	4) Skin cancer

GLOBAL WARMING

The information in a leaflet is not in a heavy block of text but broken up with:

Sub-headings (underlined)

3) numbered paragraphs

B. letters

• bullet points

* asterisks

different *styles*

different sizes

attractive pictures or diagrams

In pairs or small groups, produce a leaflet entitled 'Protect Our Wildlife' pointing out the threat posed to wild animals by human activity. List the problems under clear headings, such as speeding cars, intensive farming, pollution and litter. Make a parallel list of the solutions. Design the leaflet to be as clear and eye-catching as possible.

7.7) Listening

You are going to hear an interview with someone who is going to study bush babies in Africa. Before you listen, see if you can answer the questions below.

1 Can you tick (✔) the picture which shows a bush baby?

A ☐ B ☐ C ☐ D ☐

2 When are bush babies active?

3 What's interesting about a bush baby's nose?

4 Bush babies are related to cats. True or false?

5 What have bush babies got instead of claws?

6 How do they get from one tree to another?

7 What do they eat?

8 Do males or females have large territories?

9 Which group is sponsoring Penny's trip?

10 Why are Penny and her colleague going to record bush babies?

11 Why are they going to take samples of hair?

12 Why must Penny have rabies injections?

7.8 Hearing perception

Follow the instructions given by your teacher.

7.9 Pronunciation – linking

In spoken English, when a word begins with a vowel sound, the word before runs into it without a clear break. This is called **linking**.

Example:

it's always open   is pronounced
∘ O ∘O ∘   ∘ O ∘ O ∘
/ itsɔ:lwizəʊpən /   (itSALwaySOpen)

Listen to the tape and practise with these examples.

1 No idea. 6 Look at us.

2 Look out! 7 Not enough eggs.

3 Sooner or later. 8 Let's accept.

4 I agree. 9 All in an afternoon.

5 Not at all. 10 Give us an idea.

7.10 Review

Complete the following sentences with vocabulary from Unit 6. The first letter is given to help you.

1 There seem to be more and more 'g .... causes' asking for our money these days.

2 The people who spend most money on the lottery come from deprived a ....

3 Our monthly household i .... is getting closer and closer to our monthly outgoings.

4 The government promised a tax c .... to lower-paid workers before they were elected.

5 Investing money in the s .... market is almost always more profitable than leaving it in the bank.

6 I don't know where she got the money from but she had a wad of n .... in her handbag.

7 My firm's f .... benefits include free lunches and a car.

8 The US dollar remains the most attractive of the convertible c ....

9 The company chairman suddenly disappeared with the pension fund after he had received a b .... petition.

10 The increase in interest r .... means more and more people are having their houses repossessed.

LIST A

∘ O ∘ ∘
humanity

∘ O
request

O ∘
language

O ∘
business

∘ O ∘
expression

O ∘ ∘
lovable

∘ ∘ O ∘
entertainment

O ∘ ∘
animal

∘ ∘ O ∘
communication

∘ O
although

Shop till you drop

8.1 To start you thinking

Answer the following questions in groups.

1 What is *shoplifting*?

2 Why do you think people shoplift?

3 What would happen if you shoplifted in your own country?

8.2 Reading

a Before you read, look at the main headline.

1 What do you think the article will be about?

2 What or who do you think Tesco is?

3 What do you think *ban* means?

b Look at the second headline.

1 What has the man got to quit doing?

2 Why?

c Now read the article quickly and answer the following questions.

1 Why have Tesco banned Jim Heritage?

2 How many times has he stolen from supermarkets?

3 What is he going to do now?

TESCO BAN KING OF SHOPLIFTERS

I've got to quit after 22 years

BRITAIN'S most notorious shoplifter was banned from all of Tesco's stores yesterday.

by Nick Craven

5 Light-fingered Jim Heritage, 37, has been the scourge of supermarkets up and down the country for 22 years. He has made 20,000 illegal check-outs, been 10 prosecuted 40 times and jailed ten times.

But even being inside didn't stop his thieving. While at an open prison he would nip down to the 15 local supermarket and pinch bottles of booze for other inmates.

Hassle

Yesterday, Heritage, of Coventry, agreed to a High Court 20 order that bars him from Tesco's 500 shops nationwide.

He is already banned from all of Sainsbury's stores.

The unemployed father of two 25 claimed after yesterday's hearing he is giving up stealing – so that he can do his shopping in peace.

'It's time I went straight,' he said. 'Apart from the legal bans, 30 I've been verbally barred from my local Asda, Safeway and Morrison's stores.'

'Now it's a hassle when I want to go shopping for real and get followed around the aisles by a 35 posse of store detectives. Hopefully, other shops will realise I'm serious about giving up thieving.'

Three or four times a week, 40 Heritage would steal bottles of spirits which he later sold on.

His record haul was 189 bottles of whisky in just three hours from Tesco. 45

Unwilling to reveal his methods, he said: 'It's just a matter of having the audacity to do it.'

He added, 'It's not stealing the goods themselves or the money, 50 it's the rush of adrenalin.'

'I hope I will be able to stop now. It's like an illness, I am not proud of it.'

But Heritage aims to capitalise 55 on his life of crime by advising supermarkets on security.

'I could give an insight into how a shoplifter's mind works,' he said. 'I'd rather people came to me 60 for advice than banned me!'

8.3 Guessing vocabulary from textual links

Answer these questions about the vocabulary in the passage. Use the ideas and suggestions in brackets to help you guess the words in italics. Do not use a dictionary.

1 What do you think *light-fingered* means? (line 5)
(Why is Jim Heritage famous?)

2 *being inside* (line 12)
(Look back at the last phrase of the paragraph before.)

3 *nip down* (line 14)
(This is probably a verb of movement – but what does it mean exactly? Where was he when he went to the supermarket?)

4 *pinch* (line 15)
(Look back at paragraph 2 – what does Heritage always do when at the supermarket?)

5 *hearing* (line 25)
(Look back at line 19 to see where he was yesterday – can you guess from this what a *hearing* is?)

6 *went straight* (line 28)
(In line 26, he says he is giving up stealing.)

7 *posse* (line 36)
(In line 1, it said that Heritage was a notorious shoplifter – so how many detectives would follow him round a supermarket?)

8 *haul* (line 43)
(We know that he is a shoplifter – so what is *haul*?)

9 *the rush of adrenalin* (line 51)
(In the previous phrase, he has said he doesn't steal for the money – so what other reasons could there be?)

10 *give an insight* (line 58)
(In the previous paragraph, it says he wants to advise supermarkets on security – how could he do this?)

CHECKED OUT: Jim Heritage is banned from store

8.4 ## Grammar – past tenses for distance from reality

a Look at these examples from the newspaper article:

It's time I **went** *straight.* (line 28)

I'd rather people **came** *to me for advice than* **banned** *me.* (line 60)

What tense are the verbs in bold?
Do you think they refer to past time?

b Look at the following sentences, all of which contain the Simple Past tense. Do they refer to past time or not?

1 My mother *left* her wallet at the cash desk this morning.

2 I wish I *knew* a good place to do my Christmas shopping.

3 Supermarkets would rather you *paid* for your shopping with a credit card.

4 We *didn't find* any of the items we were looking for.

5 It's about time you *pulled* your socks up and *did* some work!

6 If you *saw* somebody leave a shop without paying, what would you do?

7 There were two men standing at the entrance who *looked* at me very suspiciously.

8 If only we *had* a bigger bag.

c Look at the sentences in part b which use an 'unreal' past tense. Write down the phrases which introduce them. Do you think they have anything in common?

d What would the people in pictures 1–10 say? Complete their sentences using a suitable verb in the past tense.

1 If only ....

2 I'd rather you ....

3 I just wish Mary ....

4 Arthur, it's high time ....

5 If only we ....

6 Wife: If you ....

7 I'm really sorry, Dad, I wish I ....

8 Come on, love, it's time ....

9 I'd rather you ....

10 If you ...., what .... ?

Discuss the following questions in groups.

1 What would you say are the main characteristics of a *department store*?

2 What differentiates a department store from
   a a supermarket?
   b an ordinary shop?
   c a shopping centre?

3 Think of a large department store you have visited. Which of the following would be found there?
   a a lift   b fruit and vegetables
   c clothes   d a toy department
   e a store guide   f a store detective
   g escalators   h showers

8.6 Vocabulary

Below you will find descriptions of ten places, objects or people that you can find in a department store or supermarket. Which is the correct word for each description?

1 A man or woman who walks around the store, pretending to be a customer, and checks people are not stealing anything.
   a store guard   b secret policeman
   c store detective

2 The place in the supermarket where you pay.
   a check-out   b pay desk
   c billing point

3 The thing with wheels that you put your purchases in.
   a supermarket trolley   b store car
   c goods buggy

4 What faces the street, and makes passers-by interested in the store?
   a street show   b window display
   c glass advertisements

5 A list of the things you can buy, and where you can find them.
   a shop map   b floor list
   c store guide

6 A part of the shop where everything is at a reduced price.
   a bargain basement   b sale section
   c offer office

7 A special place in the store where shoppers can rest and get light refreshments.
   a rest room   b snack saloon
   c coffee shop

8 The part of the store where you can buy things for children.
   a toy department   b gamestore
   c doll centre

9 A small place where you can try on clothes.
   a selection stall   b fitting room
   c test pad

10 A man or woman in uniform who walks around and looks out for thieves.
   a security guard   b store policeman
   c shop bouncer

8.7 Reading

In previous units, we have looked at ways of using discourse markers like *for example*, or conjunctions and linkers like *although* to connect phrases and sentences. Sometimes, however, a writer does not use any special words or phrases to show these links. The links should be clear **without** the linking words.

a Look at the following mini-paragraphs which are taken from larger texts. For each one, decide what is the connection between the first and the second sentence. Then rewrite each paragraph, using a conjunction or linker to show this connection.

Example:

*Popular music is the most important artistic development of the last fifty years.
I hate it.*

Connection: contrast

*Popular music is the most important artistic development of the last fifty years **but** I hate it.*

1 In parts of Wales, you can buy a five-bedroomed house for £120,000. In the south-east of England, that would just about buy you a two-up, two-down.

2 Many of the city's walls had been built at least a metre lower than they should have been. When the rains came, a flood was inevitable.

3 It was not at all surprising that the two climbers got lost. They didn't have a map, and had never been to the place before.

4 Many people lost a lot of money when the bank went down. Peter Travers, 64, from Shropshire, was forced to sell his farm and all his land.

5 Johnson's case was reported in all the papers, but only one or two included the fact that the incident happened 15 years ago. Journalists often conceal important information to make their stories more sensational or controversial.

b Read the following passage about the man who invented the department store. (The numbers down the left-hand side refer to the sentences.) Complete the text organisation chart which follows.

1
2
3
One man more than any other was responsible for the modern look of department stores. He was Harry G. Selfridge, a Wisconsin native who took a job as a stock boy with Marshall Field in 1879 and quickly rose through the ranks. One of his first acts was to take goods down from the high shelves and put them on counters and tables where customers could peer at them, touch them and, as critics noted, shoplift them (though this was by no means a new activity;

4
shoplifting has been part of the English vocabulary since 1680). Among Selfridge's many other innovations were the bargain basement, annual sales, gift certificates, the practice of reminding customers how many shopping days were left till Christmas, the custom of keeping the ground floor windows lighted at night, thus encouraging evening strollers to browse and plan their next day's shopping, and the now universal practice of putting the perfumes and cosmetics departments on the ground floor by the main entrance where they would sweeten the atmosphere and act as a magnet for passers-by.

5
6
7
8
9
10
11
12
Retiring from Marshall Field, Selfridge moved to Britain and at the age of fifty founded the London department store that bears his name. Though most British observers felt certain that such a crassly commercial undertaking would never succeed in London, it not only thrived but made Oxford Street into London's premier shopping thoroughfare. Selfridge was obsessively devoted to his store. He concerned himself with everything from the sharpness of sales clerks' pencils to the quality of their teeth. Something of his dedication to work is evidenced by a vacation he took in 1914. He left London by train on a Saturday morning and by noon the next day was on the skating-rink of a Swiss hotel. He skated vigorously for four hours, packed up his skates and stocking cap, caught a train back to London and was at his desk at 8 a.m. on the Monday morning. That was his idea of a holiday.

13, 14
15
But with the death of his wife in 1918, something snapped inside him. He began to go nightclubbing, fell in with a pair of Hungarian-American vaudeville stars known as the Dolly Sisters and neglected his business. He bought racehorses, gambled and lost spectacularly at Monte Carlo, chartered aeroplanes to bring the Dollys cartons of ice-cream and breasts of chicken for their lapdog, bought a castle on England's south coast, at Highcliffe in Hampshire, and laid plans to build a 250-room, $15 million estate nearby.

16, 17, 18
19
20
In ten years, he ran through $8 million. Unfortunately, not all of it was his. Unable to pay back the debts he owed to his own store – for a decade he and the Dollys had been helping themselves to whatever they fancied without troubling to pay for it – he was ignominiously retired from the Selfridge's board of directors and given a pension of $25,000 a year (later cut to $12,000 and then to $8,000), from which he was expected to pay back debts of $2 million. He lost his houses and his Rolls-Royce, took a small flat in Putney and travelled by bus. On 8 May 1947 he died nearly destitute and virtually forgotten, and how many times have we heard that story before?

Harry G. Selfridge

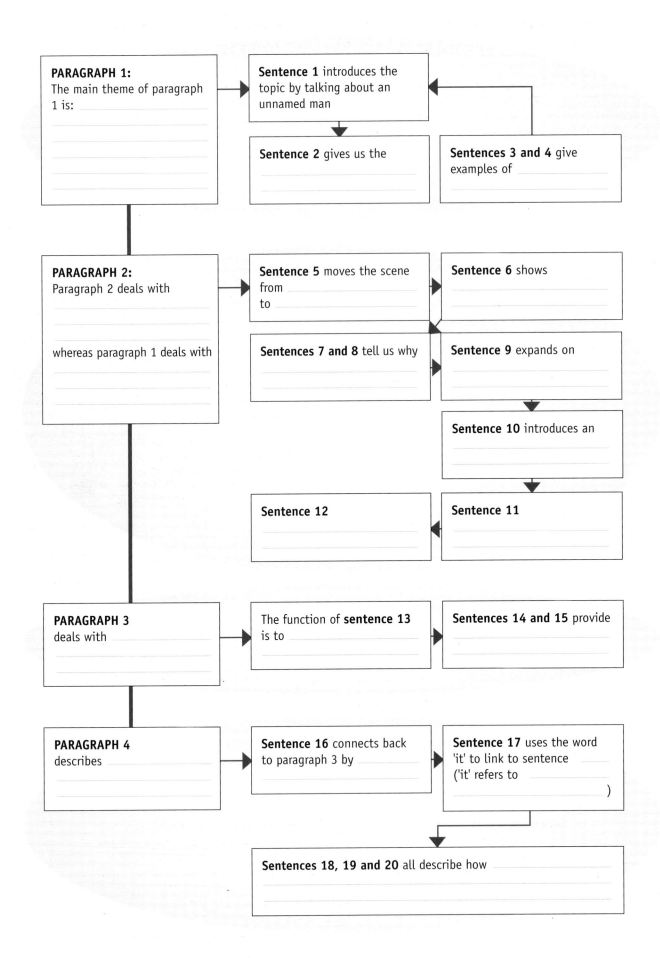

PARAGRAPH 1:
The main theme of paragraph 1 is: _____

Sentence 1 introduces the topic by talking about an unnamed man

Sentence 2 gives us the _____

Sentences 3 and 4 give examples of _____

PARAGRAPH 2:
Paragraph 2 deals with _____

whereas paragraph 1 deals with _____

Sentence 5 moves the scene from _____ to _____

Sentence 6 shows _____

Sentences 7 and 8 tell us why _____

Sentence 9 expands on _____

Sentence 10 introduces an _____

Sentence 12 _____

Sentence 11 _____

PARAGRAPH 3
deals with _____

The function of **sentence 13** is to _____

Sentences 14 and 15 provide _____

PARAGRAPH 4
describes _____

Sentence 16 connects back to paragraph 3 by _____

Sentence 17 uses the word 'it' to link to sentence _____ ('it' refers to _____)

Sentences 18, 19 and 20 all describe how _____

8.8 Writing – using examples to create coherence

Now write four paragraphs, in the same style as the passage in 8.7, about how supermarkets make you buy. Look at the following illustration, which shows a number of ways in which supermarkets make customers buy. Group the examples in the illustration into similar types and then, using the chart below the illustration, write four paragraphs. Use a dictionary for any words that you do not understand.

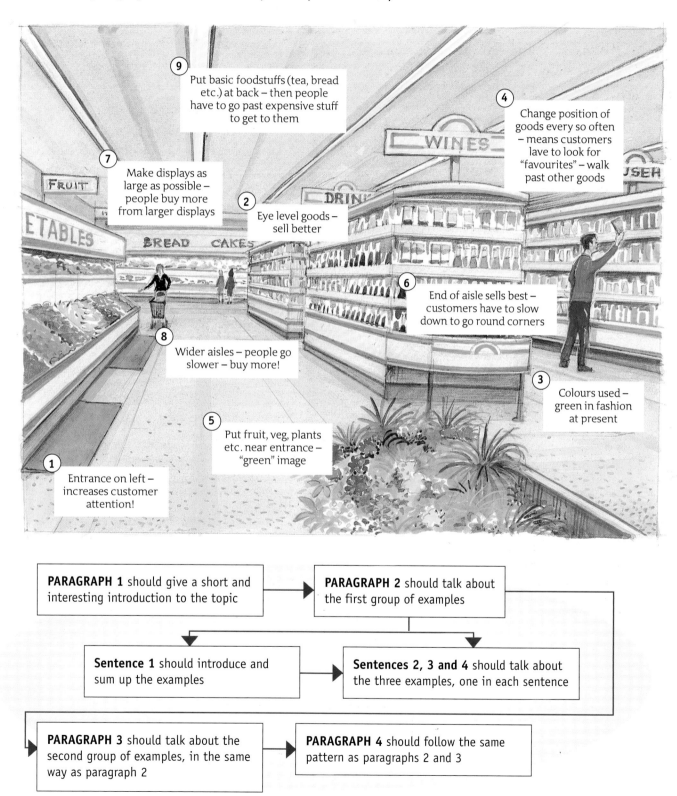

9 Put basic foodstuffs (tea, bread etc.) at back – then people have to go past expensive stuff to get to them

4 Change position of goods every so often – means customers lave to look for "favourites" – walk past other goods

7 Make displays as large as possible – people buy more from larger displays

2 Eye level goods – sell better

6 End of aisle sells best – customers have to slow down to go round corners

8 Wider aisles – people go slower – buy more!

3 Colours used – green in fashion at present

5 Put fruit, veg, plants etc. near entrance – "green" image

1 Entrance on left – increases customer attention!

PARAGRAPH 1 should give a short and interesting introduction to the topic

PARAGRAPH 2 should talk about the first group of examples

Sentence 1 should introduce and sum up the examples

Sentences 2, 3 and 4 should talk about the three examples, one in each sentence

PARAGRAPH 3 should talk about the second group of examples, in the same way as paragraph 2

PARAGRAPH 4 should follow the same pattern as paragraphs 2 and 3

8.9 Pronunciation – word-class pairs

Some words are pronounced with a different stress pattern according to whether they are nouns, adjectives or verbs.

a Listen to the six advertisements. The first time you listen, answer the question: What is each advertisement for? The second time, listen out for the following words. Decide if they are verbs, nouns or adjectives, and if the main stress is on the first or second syllable.

produce	subject	object	suspect
perfect	rebel	increase	record
convict	contract	escort	desert

b Using your answers, work out when the words are stressed on the first syllable, and when on the second.

c Say the following words according to the rules you worked out in b.

suspect (n)	perfect (v)	increase (v)
conduct (n)	protest (v)	desert (n)
upset (v)	insult (v)	convert (n)
abstract (adj)	exports (v)	present (v)

Listen to the tape and see if you were right.

d Work in pairs. Act out the following dialogues, which all contain examples of word-class pairs. Before you read, decide whether the words are nouns, verbs or adjectives, and where the stress should come.

1

SHOPKEEPER: I've decided to increase prices.

ASSISTANT: What, all the prices?

SHOPKEEPER: Yes, all the prices. Except the fresh produce.

ASSISTANT: Let's hope the customers don't protest.

2

MARKET RESEARCHER: Excuse me, Madam. I've been asked to conduct a survey into shopping habits. Would you object to answering a few questions?

SHOPPER: No, not if you're quick.

MARKET RESEARCHER: Thanks. First question: what have you bought today?

SHOPPER: I've bought an old David Bowie record called *Rebel Rebel*.

3

JANE: I've got you a present.

SOL: Wow! Nice. David Bowie. It must be twenty years old. Is it in good condition?

JANE: I think so. The man in the shop said it was perfect.

SOL: Thank you.

4

FRAN: Did you read this newspaper story about the convict?

DAN: The one who managed to shoplift even when he was in prison?

FRAN: Yes – he put the stolen objects into his prison bag!

8.10 Review

Collocation spaghetti. Each of the words and phrases around the circle can be joined to another to make a phrase which you met in Unit 7. Join up the words to make the phrases. Can you remember what they all mean?

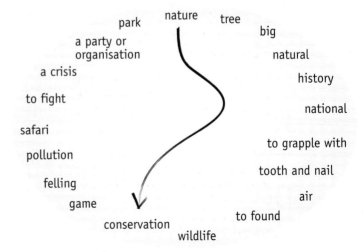

Lessons in life

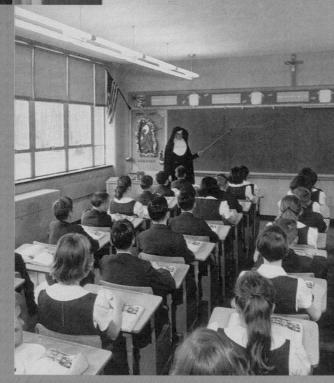

(9.1) To start you thinking

Discuss the following questions in groups.

1 What do you think 'education' is: inputting information or allowing young minds to explore?

2 What *should* it be?

3 How do you rate your school education on a scale of one to ten? Why?

4 'Education is what survives when what has been learnt has been forgotten.' Do you understand this statement? Do you agree with it?

5 Although 'education' comes from a Latin word meaning 'to draw out', nowadays it seems to mean the opposite. What do *you* think?

9.2) Reading

Look at the headings A – I, taken from the following reading passage. Read the article and choose the most suitable heading for each of the gaps numbered 1 – 6. There are more headings than you need.

A Show, don't tell.

B Give lots of praise.

C Stop buying toys.

D Watch your language.

E Listen to their questions.

F Give them time to think.

G Fly a kite.

H Direct their learning.

I Tell stories, don't recite facts.

Teach your child to WONDER

Sadly, far too few schools make science appealing. Courses introduce more new vocabulary than foreign language courses do. Textbooks are as dull as dictionaries. As a result, too many children think that science is only for people as clever as Einstein.

The irony is that children start out as natural scientists, instinctively eager to investigate the world around them. Helping them enjoy science can be easy – there's no need for a lot of scientific jargon or expensive laboratory equipment. You only have to share your children's curiosity.

Try these six simple techniques.

1

I once visited a class of seven-year-olds to talk about science as a career. The children asked me textbook questions – about schooling, salary, whether I liked my job. When I finished answering, we sat facing each other in silence. Finally I said, 'Now that we've finished with your lists, have you got any questions of your own about science?'

After a long pause, a boy raised his hand. 'Have you ever seen a grasshopper eat? When I eat leaves like that, I get stomach ache. Why?'

This began a barrage of questions that lasted nearly two hours. 'What makes tears?' 'Where do little spiders get all the stuff to make their webs?' 'Am I just a bag of blood? When I cut myself, I see blood.'

You may not know the answers to your child's questions. It's all right to say, 'I don't know but maybe we can find out.' Then you can explore the questions together.

2

Even if you know the answer to a child's question, resist the impulse to respond quickly, leaving no opening for discussion. That reinforces the misconception that science is merely a set of facts stored in the heads of adults. Science is about explaining. Science is not just facts but the meaning that people give to them – by weaving information into a story about how nature probably operates.

The best way to respond to a child's question is to begin that process of story-making together. If she asks why it's dark at night, try, 'Let's think of what is different about night that would make it darker than day'. If he wonders where bees live, say, 'Let's watch and maybe we can see where they go'. Always be ready with the answer, 'Let's find out'.

3

Grown-ups are notorious for expecting quick answers. Studies over the past three decades have shown that, after asking a question, adults typically wait only one second or less for a response – no time for a child to think. When adults increase their 'wait time' to three seconds or more, children respond with more logical, complete and creative answers.

I once conducted a lesson in air pressure by pushing two rubber toilet plungers together until all the air was driven out and they were tightly suctioned. Two children had to tug them mightily to separate them. 'How come you need so much force to pull them apart?' I asked.

After several minutes, a boy named Ron said, 'The air is trapped in there and it finds a hole and it all goes out.

9.3 Reading – interpretation

Answer the following questions, either with factual answers based on the text or by interpreting the writer's ideas.

1 Who was the article written for?

2 Why do children often give illogical or incomplete answers to adults' questions?

3 Do you think the writer of the article is a professional journalist?

4 Is the writer a man or a woman in your opinion? Why?

5 The writer thinks science is an inevitably boring subject. True or false?

6 What's wrong with saying 'Very good' when talking about science with a child?

7 What advice do you think the writer would give to school science teachers?

8 Is what the writer suggests closer to or further away from the original meaning of 'education'?

That's what makes a popping sound'. He went on to demonstrate his misconception, but I didn't say anything yet.

Another pupil then revealed what she'd been thinking: 'No, it's because all the air is *out* of the plunger'. She pushed it down on the floor until it stuck, showing that once the air was forced out of the cup, the air pressure was less on the inside than on the outside.

Rather than telling children what to think, give them time to think for themselves. If a child gets the answer wrong, be patient. You can help when needed with a few leading questions.

4

Once you have a child engaged in a science discussion, don't jump in with 'That's right' or 'Very good'. These verbal rewards work well when it comes to encouraging good behaviour. But in conversing about science, quick praise can signal that the discussion is over. Instead, keep the ball rolling by saying, 'That's interesting' or 'I'd never thought of it that way before', or coming up with more questions or ideas.

Never exhort a child to 'Think!' It doesn't make sense – children are always thinking without your telling them to.

Avoid asking 'why' questions. Most children are accustomed to hearing 'why' when their behaviour is criticised: 'Why is your bedroom so messy?' 'Why can't you behave?' Instead, I use 'How come?'

5

Real-life impressions of nature are far more memorable than any lesson children can extract from a book or TV programme. Let children look at their fingertips through a magnifying glass, and they'll understand why you want them to wash before dinner. Rather than explaining what mould is, grow some on a piece of bread. Rather than saying water evaporates, set a pan to boil and let them watch the water level drop.

If you take your children to a 'hands-on' science museum, don't manage the itinerary. Let them lead the way, and explore what interests them most.

6

Everyday activities can provide fascinating lessons in science. Children can learn a great deal about physics and engineering simply by flying a kite.

Try making your own with light-weight wood, string and paper. By the end of the afternoon's 'experiment', your children will get a basic lesson in scientific cause and effect. They'll discover how wind direction and intensity shift at different altitudes.

When buying toys, blocks of all kinds are great for construction projects. Choose toys with working parts. Even better, look for toys that children can safely take apart and put back together again.

By sharing your children's curiosity, you can give them a valuable lesson that extends far beyond the realm of science. They will learn that it pays to persist, to experiment, in the face of difficulties.

And they will see clearly that learning is not drudgery or something that happens only in school. Learning is something to be enjoyed every day – for a lifetime.

9.4 Vocabulary

In pairs, find words or phrases in the text that mean the same as or something very similar to the definitions given below.

1 a type of question in which the words used suggest the answer

2 a great number of questions suddenly directed at someone

3 special words or phrases used in a particular profession or subject (often difficult for ordinary people to understand)

4 a piece of curved glass which makes objects look larger than they really are

5 a wrong idea based on failure to understand a situation

6 the reason why something happens and the result it has

7 describing something that someone has done or used personally rather than read or learned about

8 keep doing something that you want lots of others to do

9 hard, boring work

10 soft green or grey growth that develops on old food

9.5 Reading

a Scan through the tables below from a government publication and answer the following questions.

1 Which table would you look at to find out:
   a what percentage of different countries' university students study Law and Business?
   b what students do after they graduate?
   c what percentage of 18-year-olds are either still at school or doing some form of professional training?
   d whether males or females are more likely to follow further education courses part-time?

2 Which country has the highest proportion of students taking degrees in medicine?

3 What percentage of UK first degree graduates were thought to be out of work in 1994?

TABLE A

Young people in education and training: by gender and age[1]

England						Percentages
	1990	1991	1992	1993	1994	1995
Males						
16	82	85	85	87	88	85
17	76	76	77	78	77	78
18	50	54	60	60	62	60
All males aged 16–18	68	71	73	75	76	75
Females						
16	84	88	89	90	90	88
17	68	74	77	80	79	80
18	42	44	51	57	56	59
All females aged 16–18	64	68	72	75	75	76

[1] Age at end of August. Data are at end of each year.
Source: Department for Education and Employment

Enrolments[1] in further and higher education: by type of course and gender

United Kingdom

Thousands

		Males				Females			
		1970/71	1980/81	1990/91	1994/95	1970/71	1980/81	1990/91	1994/95
Further education									
	– Full-time	116	154	219	375	95	196	261	393
	– Part-time	891	697	768	735	630	624	986	1104
Higher education									
Undergraduate	– Full-time	241	277	345	513	173	196	319	511
	– Part-time	127	176	193	210	19	71	148	273
Postgraduate	– Full-time	33	41	50	74	10	21	34	56
	– Part-time	15	32	50	92	3	13	36	84

[1] Home and overseas students. Excludes adult education centres. Includes Open University for higher education and for 1980/81

Source: Department for Education and Employment, Welsh Office,
The Scottish Office Education and Industry Department, Department of Education, Northern Ireland

TABLE B

First degree awards: by subject, international comparison, 1992

Percentages

	Medical science	Natural and physical science	Engineering and architecture	Law and business	Human sciences	All subjects
Belgium	12.8	12.1	23.9	29.3	21.9	100
Denmark	14.2	8.2	16.6	20.0	40.9	100
Germany[1]	11.7	17.6	22.2	24.7	23.7	100
Greece	10.5	16.8	13.7	12.4	46.6	100
Irish Republic	5.8	19.2	12.4	16.8	45.8	100
Italy	25.1	12.2	11.4	27.1	22.8	100
Netherlands	15.6	9.7	16.0	20.5	38.1	100
Spain	13.4	10.4	9.7	25.3	41.2	100
Sweden	17.1	12.0	16.6	23.4	31.0	100
United Kingdom	6.8	17.1	15.2	21.8	39.1	100
Australia	11.5	14.9	7.3	24.7	41.5	100
Canada	6.7	12.0	7.0	22.6	51.7	100
Japan	5.3	7.3	21.6	39.4	26.3	100
New Zealand	6.2	11.7	5.1	23.4	51.6	100
United States	7.1	10.3	8.1	27.3	47.3	100

[1] Former Federal Republic

Source: OECD

TABLE C

Destination of first degree graduates (United Kingdom)

Percentages

Year of graduation	1986[1]	1991	1993	1994
UK employment				
Permanent	50	39	39	41
Temporary	3	5	6	6
Overseas employment[2]	2	3	2	2
Further education or training	19	20	21	19
Believed unemployed	7	10	10	8
Other destinations[3]	6	10	10	10
Unknown	14	13	12	14
All first degree graduates (=100%) (thousands)	112.4	135.9	165.0	189.3

[1] Data are for Great Britain only.
[2] Home students only.
[3] Includes overseas graduates leaving the United Kingdom and graduates not available for employment.

Source: Department for Education and Employment

TABLE D

b Basing your answer on the information in the tables, complete the following passage describing trends in education.

POST-COMPULSORY EDUCATION

In the early 90s there was a strong trend towards remaining in full-time education. Around three .... (1) of those aged between sixteen and eighteen were in education and training in 1995. While the proportion of sixteen-year-olds in education and training increased only slightly between the end of 1990 and 1995, the proportion of eighteen-year-olds increased more, especially for .... (2).

For undergraduate courses, in 1994/95 there were around twice as many enrolments by men than in .... (3) and just over four times as many enrolments by women. Indeed, in 1994/95 more women enrolled on undergraduate courses than men. The increase in enrolments on postgraduate courses by women has been even sharper with an increase of over .... (4) times between 1970/71 and 1994/95.

In the United Kingdom, ... (5) was the most common subject category for first degree awards in 1992 and this was true for most other countries in the survey. Different countries had different trends. In .... (6), for example, law and business degrees accounted for almost 40% of first degree awards whilst medical science made up just .... (7) % of first degree awards, the lowest in the survey.

Just over two fifths of graduates entered permanent UK employment in .... (8). This proportion, although rising slightly in the most recent year of the survey, had dropped by about a .... (9) since 1986. Temporary employment, on the other hand, had become .... (10) as common. Around one in five graduates went on to further education or training in 1994.

9.6 Collocations and learner training

a Decide with a partner which of the following words and expressions can collocate with **school**, **education** and other connected words. Cross out those words that do not collocate and, where possible, write something that does.

1 bed and board / co-educational / one-sex **school**

2 **school** apparatus / system / year

3 **school** pupil / colleague / report

4 assist / attend / drop out of **school**

5 game / play / grammar **school**

6 private / public / state **school**

7 compulsory / obligatory / mandatory **education**

8 further / supplementary / higher **education**

9 do / have / make **lessons**

10 make / follow / take **a course**

b Now make your own keyword grids for **school** and **education** using the words above and others you find in your dictionary.

Verbs	Describing words	Keyword	Words that come after
		school	
		education	

C Based on your grids, complete the following sentences with suitable collocations (two words or more) with **school** and **education**.

1 .... schools are for children over eleven of all abilities.

2 I've lost touch with most of my old school .... , except for Phil.

3 The name .... school is very illogical since it means a private school for the children of the rich and privileged.

4 People always insist that your school .... are the happiest of your life!

5 The British .... system comes in for a lot of criticism in the report.

6 The school- .... in Britain and Australia is the same – sixteen.

7 As every school .... knows, oil floats on water.

8 Primary .... in Britain generally lasts from age five to eleven.

9.7 Writing – adding detail

Adding detail is a very important way of giving colour to your writing. Giving concrete examples can also relate your arguments to the real world. Writing with no detail tends to be boring for the reader.

Look at the following outline of a primary school experience. Where there are gaps, add the missing factual information for yourself. Where there are asterisks, add one or two sentences which give interesting details.

> When I was .... years old I went to a primary school*, or .... as it's called in my country.
>
> My first day at school* was
>
> ....
>
> I met a lot of other kids at school but I had one particular friend*.
>
> ....
>
> We used to play different games* during the breaks between lessons.
>
> ....
>
> I can still remember our class teacher*.

9.8 Grammar – *any* and *some*

a Look at these two examples from the reading passage in 9.2.

1 *... have you got **any** questions of your own ...?*

2 *Real-life impressions are far more memorable than **any** lesson children can extract from a book ...*

These two examples show different uses of *any*. In the first example, the common rule applies: *any* in questions and negatives and *some* in affirmatives. In the second example, the rule does not apply. Conclusion: the rule is only partially true.

Now look at these more useful rules, and match them with the correct examples of how *any* and *some* are really used below. Some examples may match with more than one rule.

A A part or the whole

- When we are talking about a limited number of the things, or part of the things being referred to, we use *some* in negatives and affirmatives.

- When we are talking about all of the things, or the whole of the thing, being referred to, we use *any* in negatives or affirmatives with a negative meaning/message. (In normal affirmatives, we use *all* rather than *any*.)

B Choice

- When we are talking about an unlimited choice from a selection of things, or we are excluding choice completely, we use *any*.

- When we are emphasising that the choice is limited, we use *some*.

C In questions

- We often use *any* if the existence of what we are referring to is in doubt.

- We often use *some* if we are referring to something that obviously exists.

D Expected answers

- If we expect the answer *yes*, we use *some* in questions or offers.

- If we expect the answer *no*, or don't know what to expect, we use *any* in questions or offers.

- We normally use *some* rather than *any* in requests.

1 I don't like some of the teachers at my college.

2 I'm sure that any tutor you appoint will be fine.

3 Can I have some more paper, please?

4 Are there any board pens in the classroom?

5 Would you like any help with your assignment? Or are you determined to do it on your own?

6 Would you like some help with that – it's a bit difficult, isn't it?

7 My tutor never gives me any help.

8 Write 5,000 words on any topic you like.

9 The professor refused to allow the use of any type of calculator in the exam.

10 You can borrow some of the books in the library, but many are just for reference.

11 I'll be surprised if he passes any of his exams – he's bound to fail them all if you want my opinion.

12 I know you said the Course Requirements demand 100% attendance, but could I miss some classes next week, please?

b In which sentences is it possible to use only *some*, in which only *any*, and in which both? Where both are possible, what is the difference in meaning?

1 I'm not very keen on *any/some* classical music.

2 Have you got *any/some* old text books you could let us have?

3 Did you want *any/some* extra homework?

4 Sorry, I can't help you – I don't have *any/some* information on that.

5 Oh, come on, Dad. I've got to have *any/some* money for the school trip. Can't you lend me ten pounds?

6 Computers are getting easier to use. If you don't believe me, ask *any/some* school kid.

7 He's useless, he never answers *any/some* questions in a way we can understand!

8 The art teacher absolutely adores *any/some* modern architecture.

9 Shouldn't there be *any/some* instructions for this equipment in the box?

10 I think I'll put the students' paintings up on the wall. Pass me *any/some* of those drawing pins, would you?

C Complete these sentences with *any* or *some*.

1 I don't suppose you've finished with .... of the notes I lent you, have you?

2 The head asked me to help mark your students' exam papers. Can you give me .... now? I'll make a start on them.

3 I didn't go to .... of the lectures last term, but the ones I attended seemed to cover all the topics listed in the course outline anyway.

4 Are you going to lead .... of the seminars this term like we agreed?

5 I'll assist you in .... way I can.

(9.9) Listening

Read the following questions, then listen to these extracts from three interviews and answer the questions.

1 What is Thomas' surname?

2 What sort of primary school did he attend?

3 What are the main goals of Summerhill school?

4 What does Claire think of the teachers at her school?

5 What is her opinion of more 'conventional' schools?

6 What is Chris' opinion of the teachers he had at school?

7 Why didn't he find geometry appealing?

8 What does he do now?

9 Who went to a co-educational school?

10 Who seems most bitter about their school days?

(9.10) Review ⏪

Complete the following short story. Use the words from Unit 8 in the box below which mean the same as the words in brackets. You may have to change the tense of some verbs.

> store detective   pinch   inside   nip
> straight   fitting room   checkout
> trolley   claim   light-fingered

Gavin's always been a bit .... (1) (steals habitually) and has been .... (2) (in jail) several times. On one famous occasion, he told Maria, his wife, he was going to .... (3) down (visit quickly) to the supermarket to do a bit of shopping. Half an hour later he came back home with a .... (4) (basket on wheels) full of food that he'd just .... (5) (stolen)! Maria had been trying to make him go .... (6) (honest) and was pretty angry with him. Of course, Gavin .... (7) (said) there had been nobody at the supermarket .... (8) (place where you pay) so he'd thought it was all right just to walk out!

On another occasion, he was caught leaving a .... (9) (where you try clothes on) wearing five jackets!

It's hardly surprising that almost every .... (10) (person who watches out for thieves in a shop) in the local area now calls the police as soon as Gavin walks in!

Read all about it!

To start you thinking

Discuss the following questions in groups.

1 What is the difference between a *tabloid* and a *broadsheet* newspaper?

2 Do you have a similar difference in the newspapers in your country?

3 When you are reading the two types of newspapers in English, which do you find more difficult to understand?

4 Look back at the article 'TESCO ban…' on page 76. Do you think it comes from a tabloid or a broadsheet? Why?

Reading

You are going to read two articles from different newspapers, one from a tabloid and one from a broadsheet, which deal with the same news item.

a Before you read the two articles, look at the two headlines and answer the questions.

1 What are *joyriders*?

2 What has happened?

3 Which headline was in the *Mirror* (the tabloid) and which in the *Guardian* (the broadsheet)?

1

Car driven by boy, 12, crashes in flames

2

JOYRIDERS AGED 8 AND 12 IN 70MPH SMASH

b Read through the articles quickly, and note down three pieces of information which are in **both** articles.

ARTICLE 1

By STEPHEN WHITE

POLICE who dragged two joyriders from a blazing car yesterday were amazed to discover the driver was aged TWELVE and his passenger was EIGHT.

The step-brothers sneaked out of bed in the middle of the night, nicked a Vauxhall Cavalier and were chased at speeds of up to 70 mph before smashing into a wall. Their lives were saved by PC Simon Waddington, 32, and WPC Jackie Pendlebury, 29, who smashed the side windows and pulled them clear as flames engulfed the car. The driver, barely able to reach the pedals, escaped with minor cuts.

But his young brother suffered serious spine and stomach injuries and was in intensive care last night. Their father said: 'I don't know how they managed to start the car.'

Dumped

'Normally they are good lads who like to play football in the garden.'

A senior police officer warned: 'It is typical of the worrying and sad trend of younger and younger people going out and committing offences like this.'

The F reg Cavalier was stolen on Saturday night and dumped in Salford, Greater Manchester, where the two tearaways found it.

Police in a Transit van gave chase after spotting the car at 3.40 a.m., when it was driven the wrong way along a dual carriageway.

The Cavalier failed to take a bend, ploughed into the wall of a disused pub and burst into flames with the youngsters trapped. Witness Mark Harris said: 'They must have been doing 70 mph.'

The children, from Salford, have not been named. The eight-year-old is too young to be prosecuted.

ARTICLE 2

David Ward

A 12-year-old boy was driving a stolen car when it crashed into a building and burst into flames in Salford, Greater Manchester, early yesterday.

Two police officers pulled him from the crashed vehicle, along with his eight-year-old step-brother, a passenger in the car.

The boys were taken to hospital, where the younger one is in intensive care with serious back and internal injuries. The 12-year-old sustained only cuts and bruises.

Constables Nick Waddington, aged 32, and Jackie Pendlebury, 29, who were on a routine patrol in a police van, began to trail the Vauxhall Cavalier when they saw it being driven erratically down the wrong side of a dual carriageway at 3.40 a.m.

The 12-year-old accelerated away and tried to turn right. But the car crashed into the wall of a derelict pub and caught fire.

The officers smashed the car's windows and pulled the boys out.

The car had been stolen in Stretford, Greater Manchester, at the weekend and is believed to have been abandoned after being used in a crime in north Manchester.

The boys' father said later that they must have sneaked out of the house at 3 a.m.

He added, 'I don't know how they managed to start the car. They have never done anything like this before. Normally they are good lads who like to play football in the back garden with the other kids.'

A man who lives near the accident scene said: 'I saw the officers trying to smash the windows to get the kids out of the car. A lot of other police officers turned up. One of the boys was out cold on the floor. They managed to sit the other one up against a wall of the pub.'

Superintendent Phil Hollowood, based at Salford, said the two constables had probably saved the boys' lives. 'The officers, with little regard for their own safety, went up to the car despite the heat and the flames, broke in and released two young boys, thereby preventing far more serious injury.'

The circumstances of the incident are to be investigated by an officer from another force, according to standard procedure.

The 12-year-old was allowed home after treatment but the eight-year-old remains in intensive care at the Royal Manchester children's hospital. Police are waiting to interview both boys.

c Now read the articles again in detail. Do not work on the vocabulary at this stage. Answer the following questions.

1 Which do you think is the better headline?

2 The following pieces of information are in one of the articles, but not the other. Which articles are they from?

 a the boys were doing 70

 b the witness's statement

 c the name of the police officer who spoke to the press

 d the eight-year-old is too young to be prosecuted

 e the police will investigate

 f where the children come from

 g the police's warning that younger and younger people are committing offences

 h the police will interview the children

 i the age of the car

3 What effect do these pieces of information have on each article?

4 What similarities are there between the two versions?

5 In your opinion, do you think the two pieces are generally organised in a similar way to each other, or a different way?

6 Which of the two pieces do you find easier to understand?

d The two articles use different vocabulary items to express the same facts. Using a dictionary, match the phrasing from the *Mirror* article on the left with that of the *Guardian* article on the right.

1	dragged (line 1)	a	stolen (line 2)
2	ploughed into (line 29)	b	crashed into (line 3)
3	gave chase (line 26)	c	caught fire (line 30)
4	nicked (line 6)	d	derelict (line 30)
5	driven the wrong way (line 27)	e	despite the heat and the flames (line 65)
6	smashing into (line 8)	f	crashed into (line 29)
7	spot(ting) (line 26)	g	driven erratically down the wrong side (line 23)
8	disused (line 30)	h	police officers/ constables (lines 7 and 18)
9	dumped (line 24)	i	saw (line 23)
10	tearaways (line 25)	j	pulled (line 32)
11	PC + WPC (line 9)	k	abandoned (line 37)
12	burst into flames (line 30)	l	trail (line 22)
13	flames engulfed the car (line 11)	m	lads (line 47)

e What are the differences between the two newspapers' use of vocabulary, and what is the general effect of these differences?

10.3 Vocabulary

In order to avoid repetition, writers often use a different word or phrase to refer to the same thing. Look at these examples from the stories:

*Police who dragged two joyriders from a blazing **car** yesterday... The **Cavalier** failed to take a bend...* (article 1, lines 1 and 29)

*Two **police officers** pulled him... **Constables** Nick Waddington and Jackie Pendlebury...* (article 2, lines 7 and 18)

a Look at the following extracts. In the second one of each pair, there is a word or phrase or name which refers back to the first. Draw an arrow from the word or phrase in the second sentence to the one in the first sentence, as in the example. The word may refer to a proper name somewhere else in the paragraph.

1

Taylor Touchstone drifted off downstream as his family and some friends held a picnic near Pensacola in Florida. The ten-year-old boy was lost in the Gulf Coast swamplands for four days.

2

Two Albanian towns were blacked out for several hours last June when a mouse chewed through a cable causing a short circuit and sparked a £7,000 power plant blaze. The fire burned down a high-voltage distribution centre in the town of Kruja...

3

I travelled the next day to Salzburg. I found it hard to warm to, which surprised me because I had fond, if somewhat hazy, memories of the place.

4

Sue Phillips returned home in the early hours to find a group of five white men, all wearing dark woolly hats, having a drinks party in her flat in Tilbury, Essex. One of them asked the astonished woman to dance.

5

A pilot, who had a miracle escape when his helicopter crashed, fell out of the army helicopter that rescued him. A major search was organised to find Luis Eduardo Iglesias, who fell out of the chopper in the mountains of Tolima province in south-western Colombia.

6

A young German couple fled their home after a musical greetings card slipped down behind a cupboard and fell into a wall cavity, where it kept playing night and day for four months. Anneliese and Axel Probst called in a builder, who said he would have to knock the wall down, but they couldn't afford the £1,200 cost. So they moved in with relatives until the electronic chip ran out of power.

b In the two newspaper stories in 10.2, there are examples of the writer referring to the same thing or person in two or more different ways, including proper names. Find as many examples as you can.

c In the following text, there are a number of repetitions, which make it rather uninteresting to read. Go through the text and underline the repetitions – the first has been done as an example. Then rewrite the text, avoiding repetitions.

KENNETH BLAKE, a 36-year-old company director from London, was rescued from muggers – by a 74-year-old woman!

5 <u>Blake</u> was walking alone in Ealing when two muggers, believed to be in their teens, accosted him in the street. 'I was pretty scared,' said Blake, 'as I thought they might have knives. Luckily help was at hand.'

10 Help was in the form of Edith Howarth who had seen the incident from the other side of the street. She crossed the street, shouted at the muggers, and started beating them over the head with her walking stick. 'Ealing is usually a very quiet place,' she said later, 15 'and we don't want it to change. We have to stop muggers if we can.'

Edith was later praised by the police. 'We believe it is the duty of people to help each other as much as possible in situations like 20 these. This incident just shows that age is not really important.'

The muggers ran away, but were later arrested. Police believe they were behind a series of incidents in Ealing. They were not 25 carrying any knives.

EDITH HOWARTH - Praised by police

10.4 Grammar – using participles

a Look at the examples of participles from the reading text in 10.2 and match them with the descriptions of use below.

1 The F reg Cavalier **was stolen** on Saturday night and **dumped** in Salford… (line 23)

2 The Cavalier… burst into flames with the youngsters **trapped**. (line 29)

3 The children, from Salford, have not **been named**. (line 33)

4 A 12-year-old boy was **driving** a **stolen** car… (line 1)

5 Two police officers pulled him from the **crashed** vehicle… (line 7)

6 …they saw it **being driven** erratically… (line 23)

7 I saw the officers **trying** to smash the windows… (line 51)

Three common uses of participles are:

a) to form the continuous aspect (present participle), the perfect aspect and passive constructions (past participle).

b) as adjectives.

c) to give information about the actions of the object of the sentence, especially verbs of sense (*see, hear, smell,* etc.). (Called object complements.)

b Participles are also used to make adverbial clauses, saying why, when or how something happened. Decide if the examples below describe why, when or how, and if they are using present or past participles.

1 Twisting a coat-hanger into the keyhole, the prisoner managed to open the door.

2 Being surrounded by the police, she hid the drugs.

3 Before leaving the house, they always switched on their burglar alarm.

Perfect participles can be active or passive, and are often used to talk about why or when. Decide if the examples below describe why or when, and if they are active or passive.

4 Having broken into the vault, the thieves began to remove the gold.

5 Having been robbed several times, she always avoided walking home alone at night.

c Now shorten or join the sentences using present, past or perfect participles.

1 The vandals were smashing all the windows in the sports pavilion. The watchman saw them.

2 The crooks felt confident of getting away with their crime because they had destroyed the evidence.

3 The minister was forced to resign because he was caught with stolen documents.

4 There were explosives hidden in the luggage. The sniffer dogs could smell them.

5 The suspect sobbed uncontrollably as she insisted that she was innocent.

6 The rioter was handcuffed. Then she was unable to resist arrest.

7 Everyone could hear the police sirens. The sound was getting closer!

8 The escaped convict thought he was likely to be captured. For that reason, he hid in a barn for six days.

(10.5) Listening

a Words can be put into three categories:

1 words which are only used in informal situations (e.g. two friends talking in a cafe);

2 words which are only used in formal situations (e.g. a customer talking to her bank manager);

3 words which can be used in both informal and formal situations – so-called 'neutral' vocabulary.

Look at the following list of words and phrases, all of which come from the stories in 10.2, and put them into one of the three categories above. Use a dictionary for those words you do not know.

sneaked out	nicked	escaped
minor	father	lads
offences	witness	police officers
vehicle	prosecuted	internal injuries
sustained	kids	out cold
thereby		

b You are going to listen to a man telling a story. The story features all the objects in the drawings. In groups, try to predict how the story will unfold.

c Read the following statements, then listen to the story. As you listen, decide if the statements are true or false.

1 The man is probably telling the story to a friend.

2 He has had a problem with something he bought.

3 He complained immediately.

4 The little girl found something strange in the packet.

5 Her brother was most distressed.

6 This incident has happened before.

7 The man is planning to write to the company which made the product.

d Listen to the piece again, and change the following informal words and phrases from the text into neutral and/ or formal ones. Say if the new words are neutral or formal. The first one has been done as an example.

1 kids

     children (neutral)

2 starving

3 daylight robbery

4 yucky

5 make a fuss

6 stuff

7 know what I mean?

8 hacked off

9 she's **down** two Supahoops

10 her **little** brother

11 he's laughing his head off!

12 the thing is

13 week in week out

14 **get** her another packet

15 better still

16 dosh

10.6 Writing – choosing correct register

a When someone tells a story to their friends, they often use informal words and phrases, such as in the story you listened to in 10.5c. You are going to write to the crisp company mentioned in the story. Look at the following informal words and phrases from that story, and decide how you would re-write them in a more appropriate register.

1 I don't know how to describe it really

2 a piece of crisp stuff… **like** someone's dropped…

3 we've been… for **years**

4 never anything wrong before

5 make it up to her

b Words and phrases in English can be divided into three categories: formal, informal and neutral. It is not always necessary to write in as formal a style as possible, because sometimes this can sound pompous or rude, or even as if you are making fun of the person you are writing to. At the same time, it is important to avoid language which is too informal.

Read the letter of complaint to Supahoops. The writer has sometimes used language which is inappropriate. Suggest alternatives. The first one has been done as an example.

141, Winkfield Road
Wood Green
London N22 5HZ

Dear Friend Sir/Madam,

I am just writing to complain about a packet of
Supahoops which I purchased in a shop in Wood Green
London.

On 12 February, I bought a couple of packets of
Supahoops for my two offspring. While my three-year-
old was consuming her hoops, she came across a nasty
finger-shaped thing with spots on it. You will understand
that she was pretty distressed by this. It was quite a
shock for us, as we have been buying your stuff for ages,
and have always been delighted with them.

I've put the Supahoop in with this letter, along with the
packet. This might assist you to analyse it and thus to
prevent a re-occurrence of the problem.

Finally, I am confident you would agree with me that a
reimbursement of our money would be just right.

I am looking forward to hearing from you forthwith,

Best wishes,

(10.7) Hearing perception

Follow the instructions given by your teacher.

(10.8) Review ◀◀

Complete the crossword. All the words and phrases come from Unit 9.

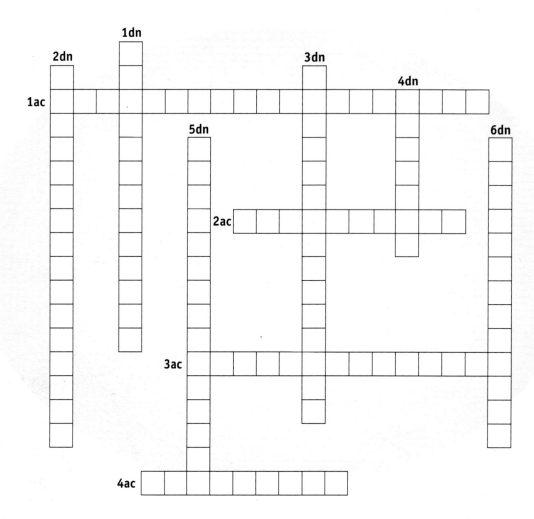

CLUES

Across (ac)

1 A school with both boys and girls. (13,6)

2 A school for children aged three to five. (10)

3 When one thing happens as a result of another, we say it is… (5,3,6)

4 A … school is one with only girls or only boys. (6,3)

Down (dn)

1 A student who is doing a university course for a first degree. (13)

2 Special language which scientists use when talking to each other. (10,6)

3 A thing you can look through which makes things look bigger. (10,5)

4 An adjective which means providing practical experience of something, not just information. (5,2)

5 A general term for universities (and colleges) for over-eighteens. (6,9)

6 An idea which is wrong, based on a failure to understand. (13)

Living in the city

(11.1) ## To start you thinking

Discuss these questions in groups.

1   What's your favourite city? Why?

2   What are the characteristics of a pleasant city?

3   What makes a city pleasant (or unpleasant) to live in? Make a list of ten features.

4   Think of a city you know well. How many of the ten features does it possess?

11.2 Reading

a Read the following questions, then quickly skim the six pieces about cities and answer the questions:

1 Which are about a particular city, and which are about cities in general?

2 Can you guess which cities are being talked about? Choose from this list:

Istanbul New York Cairo Paris
London Johannesburg Barcelona

3 Where might each piece come from? Choose from this list:

travel writing in a newspaper
a lyrical description
a tourist guidebook
a history of a city
a book about town planning
memories of a city childhood
a novel
a social history book
words of a song

b Scan the pieces again and find the answers to these questions.

1 Which century is the Enlargement associated with?

2 Where can you buy books at 10 p.m.?

3 How many edge cities does America now have?

4 What happened in 969 AD?

5 What's the rhyme scheme of the poem?

6 Why is 1850 an important date in the history of urban development?

1

Like Venice, Al Qahira has an elegant simplicity of design which makes for clarity of purpose. It was conceived as a fortified palace compound: the palaces have vanished, but the rectangular ground plan remains much as it was when the Caliph's Moroccan   5 astrologers declared it propitious in 969 AD.

Among the tangled maze of alleys a single main artery passes, with several changes of name. It runs from Bab Zuweila to Bab Futuh, from the southern gate to the northern, following an immemorial   10 caravan route to the Red Sea. This was always the principal street of Grand …, one of the great thoroughfares of the world, certainly one of the most resilient, and the true locale of the Thousand and One Nights – ostensibly set in Baghdad but really a   15 reflection of this tremendous oriental capital.

About half-way along stands the great bazaar quarter, Khan el Khalil, as magnetic a focus for tourists today as it was seven centuries ago for the turbaned merchants of the eastern world – still   20 gleaming with gold and silver, rich with carpets, sickly with perfumes and cluttered with souvenirs ghastly and alluring. It forms a compact if labyrinthine quarter of its own: the medieval equivalent of a mall, and the well-defined focus   25 of commercial life in the city.

2

Composed upon …, September 3, 1802

Earth has not anything to show more fair:
Dull would he be of soul who could pass by
A sight so touching in its majesty:
This City now doth, like a garment, wear
The beauty of the morning; silent, bare,   5
Ships, towers, domes, theatres, and temples lie
Open unto the fields, and to the sky;
All bright and glittering in the smokeless air.

Never did sun more beautifully steep
In his first splendour, valley, rock, or hill;   10
Ne'er saw I, never felt, a calm so deep!
The river glideth at his own sweet will:
Dear God! the very houses seem asleep;
And all that mighty heart is lying still!

3

... is really three cities, sharply distinct in character, the newest enclosing the older, in which the oldest is set. On the perimeter, laced with ribbons of freeway, are the industrial suburbs that grew up in the post-1945 years of the Franco dictatorship; they are the products of unconstrained, unplanned growth in the 1950s and 1960s, stretching south to the Llobregat and north to the Besos rivers – a sprawl of factories and polygons, housing blocks for hundreds and thousands of migrant workers who flooded ... and decisively changed its social mix. Inside that is the big nineteenth-century grid of the Eixample, or Enlargement, which occupies the coastal plain where the massif breaks away and slopes down to the Mediterranean: the New City, a repetitive carpet of squares with chamfered corners, slit by larger avenues, all laid out on paper in 1859 and mostly filled in by 1910. Then, inside that, where the grid meets the bay, you see the regular march of units break up, bunch into confusion, and become an irregular cell cluster from which older-looking protrusions rise: old square towers, Gothic peaks. This is the Old City, the Barri Gotic, or Gothic Quarter. To the right of it, the mountain of Montjuic rises. Beyond Montjuic lies the flat plain of the Mediterranean, silky, blue, and glittering. Inland ridge, plain, mountain, sea: the elements from which the city's life was shaped.

4

Even then, Chelsea was a sociable part of ..., and Singleton and her friends would constantly be in and out of each other's flats and houses. Some of this familiarity was born out of the architecture. 'In the houses where I was living, nobody had individual flats,' she says. 'So if you lived at the top you would walk through other people's homes.' It was not until the building boom of the seventies that houses were transformed into proper flats.

Like many parts of ... in the fifties and the early sixties, there was not much entertainment in Chelsea. It had an almost suburban feel. 'If you wanted to go to a decent restaurant or to see a play, you had to go to the West End,' Singleton recalls. 'Somehow ... was so small then, and there were so many fewer people that you would actually bump into people you knew in the West End. What I love about Chelsea now is that you can walk along the Fulham Road and buy books at 10 p.m. There's also a lovely burgeoning of cafes. In one I go to, I have begun to make new friends.'

5

But, as seen in Chapter 1, after 1850 a profound change came over the centres of the metropolitan cities: the traditional activities were joined, and then even sometimes displaced, by new types of activity which were characteristically carried on in offices. This was no sudden once-for-all process; it has gone on happening ever since, and it threatens to be a major feature of the development of the great metropolitan centres in the immediate future. Indeed, the process may be speeding up; the 1960s and 1970s have seen a radical reconstruction of factory industry in most advanced industrial countries, leading first to great advances in productivity that actually reduced total manufacturing employment and, second, to a movement of that employment to suburban and smaller city sites. But, since the process was part and parcel of a profound change in the international division of labour, this decline in the manufacturing base of the advanced industrial cities has no parallel in the cities of the developing world; there, the processes of industrialization and urbanization in the third world – vast, willing, weakly-organised labour force willing to accept work at low wages, coupled with a buccaneer entrepreneurial quality – acted to bring about the contraction of industry in the first world.

6

To qualify as an edge city by Garreau's definition, a community must have five million square feet of office space, 600,000 square feet of shopping, and more people working there than living there. America now has more than 200 edge cities. Los Angeles and New York have about two dozen each. Almost all have been created since 1960, and almost always they are soulless, impersonal places, unfocused collections of shopping malls and office complexes that are   5
ruthlessly unsympathetic to non-motorists. Many have no pavements or pedestrian crossings, and only rarely do they offer any but the most skeletal public transport links to the nearby metropolis, effectively denying job opportunities to many of those left behind in the declining inner cities. About one-third of all Americans now live in edge cities, and up to two-thirds of Americans work in them. They are substantial places, and yet most people outside their   10
immediate areas have never heard of them. How many Americans, I wonder, could go to a map and point to even the general location of Walnut Creek, Rancho Cucamonga, Glendale, Westport Plaza, Mesquite or Plano? Anonymous or not, they are the wave of the future. In 1993, nineteen of the twenty-five fastest-growing communities in the United States were edge cities.

(11.3) Vocabulary

a Working in groups, find the following adjectives in the texts. In this context, do they denote the author's approval, disapproval or neither?

Text 1	Text 2	Text 3	Text 4	Text 5	Text 6
tangled (line 7)	touching (line 3)	distinct (line 2)	sociable (line 1)	profound (line 2)	soulless (line 4)
resilient (line 14)	silent (line 5)	unplanned (line 11)	individual (line 8)	traditional (line 3)	impersonal (line 5)
tremendous (line 16)	deep (line 11)	repetitive (line 29)	proper (line 13)	radical (line 12)	skeletal (line 7)
magnetic (line 18)		irregular (line 38)	suburban (line 17)	industrial (line 14)	substantial (line 10)
sickly (line 22)		silky (line 47)	small (line 21)	suburban (line 18)	anonymous (line 13)
ghastly (line 23)				vast (line 25)	fastest-growing (line 14)
compact (line 23)				weakly-organised (line 25)	
labyrinthine (line 24)				buccaneer (line 27)	
commercial (line 26)					

b Take five of the words which show disapproval or a neutral attitude. Can you think of a context where they could be used approvingly? For each one, write a sentence to show how.

c Now take five of the words which show approval or a neutral attitude. Can you think of contexts where they could show disapproval?

11.4 Collocations

a Look at the following list of collocations from the six texts.

1 ground plan
2 main artery
3 industrial suburbs
4 housing blocks
5 social mix
6 office space
7 office complexes
8 shopping mall
9 pedestrian crossing
10 public transport
11 inner city
12 immediate areas
13 industrial countries
14 developing world
15 labour force

Match the collocations above with the definitions below. Write the number of the collocation after the correct definition. The first one has been done as an example.

a buildings, or groups of buildings, or an area, containing many offices

b the workers in a company

c a special place for people to walk across the road

d big or principal road

e rooms in a building which can be rented to use as an office

f outlying districts of a town or city where there are factories, etc.

g a drawn plan of a building at ground level .....1....

h the various different types of people who live or work in a place

i the central part of a city, especially a part with a large (usually poor) population, old buildings in bad condition, etc.

j bus and train systems owned by city or state authorities

k the poorer countries of the world

l a large shopping centre, often enclosed, where cars are not allowed

m countries where industry and technology are well-developed

n the nearest areas to something

o large or tall buildings where people live

b In boxes 1–8 below, one word from the list in part a can go in each space to form several different collocations. Using a good monolingual dictionary, look up the first words in the collocations above, and decide which one can go in each of the boxes.

1		hall
town		house
		planning
		centre

2		concern
		action
		future
		family

3		block
		boy
		equipment
		hours

4		address system
		corporation
		enemy
		house
		relations
		school
		opinion
		library
		convenience

5	
....	services security worker conscience life club climber science

6	
....	floor rule sheet staff work

7	
....	relations action estate revolution

8	
....	conditions policy association estate

C Choose ten of the collocations from part b which you think will be most useful to you. Think of a strategy for remembering them in future.

11.5 Grammar – positions of adverbs

a Look at these examples from the texts in 11.2. The words in brackets have been taken out. Put them back in the right place.

1 (*always*) This was the principal street of Grand Cairo… (text 1)

2 (*in the 1950s and 1960s*) … they are the products of unconstrained, unplanned growth… (text 3)

3 (*constantly*) Singleton and her friends would be in and out of each other's flats and houses. (text 4)

4 (*actually*) … great advances in productivity that reduced total manufacturing employment… (text 5)

b Answer the questions in the adverb and adverbial phrase quiz.

1 Where in the sentence can you put these adverbs of frequency? Which adverb behaves differently from the others?

always   usually   often   never

Tourists visit the new shopping mall.

2 Where in the sentences can you put these adverbs of certainty? What is the difference between their position in affirmative and negative sentences?

probably   possibly   definitely

a The planning officer has gone to a council meeting.

b The planning officer hasn't gone to a council meeting.

3 How are the positions of adverbs of frequency and adverbs of manner affected by the sentence being affirmative or negative?

always   slowly

Attitudes to high-rise housing are changing.

Attitudes to high-rise housing aren't changing.

4 Where in the sentences can you put these adverbs of manner?

quickly   slowly   fast   well

a   The town developed.

b   The town developed into a city.

c   The town developed its industry.

5 Put these adverbial phrases into the sentence. Do they come before or after the adverb of manner? If you put both phrases into the sentence together, which comes before the other?

in the 1980s   across the whole region

The anti-road lobby presented its arguments carefully.

6 Look at the possible positions of the adverbs in the sentences below. All of them are correct, but they change the meanings of the sentences. Explain how.

a   (• = *only*) • Frances had • seen • the • planning report.

b   (• = *secretly*) The committee • arranged to view the new public statue •.

(11.6)   Learner training

a Read the sentences and identify the mistake in each one. Then look at the following extract from the index of a grammar reference book and decide in which section you would look to help you with the mistakes.

1 Traffic always has a negative affect on city life.

2 They live in a brick red house.

3 We enjoyed the party very much, and after we got a taxi home.

4 The library will close on March.

5 It seems that some problems have risen with the new by-pass.

List of Entries

b You are going to concentrate on the difference between adverbs and adjectives. Study the following extracts from a different grammar reference book.

UNIT 84

Adjectives and adverbs

A

We use an **adverb**, not an **adjective**
- to say *how* something happened or was done:
  - I've always **greatly** enjoyed his novels. (*not* ...great enjoyed...)
  - The people who work in that shop always talk **politely** to customers. (*not* ...polite...)
- to modify adjectives, including participle adjectives (see Unit 85):
  - It was **strangely** *quiet* in the room.   • They had a **beautifully** *furnished* house.

B

Some adverbs are formed from **an adjective + -ly: happy → happily,** etc. When an adjective already ends in -ly (e.g. **cowardly, friendly, kindly, lively, lonely**) we don't add -ly to it to make an adverb. Instead we can use a prepositional phrase with **fashion, manner,** or **way:**
  - He smiled at me in **a friendly way.**   • She waved her hands around in **a lively fashion.**

Most participle adjectives ending in -ed (see Unit 85) don't have an adverb form and we can use a similar prepositional phrase:
  - They rose to greet me **in a subdued manner.**
  - She walked around the room **in an agitated way.** (*or* ...**in agitation.**)

However, some do have an adverb form with -ly, including the following common ones: **allegedly, belatedly, contentedly, dejectedly, deservedly, excitedly, hurriedly, markedly, pointedly, repeatedly, reportedly, reputedly, supposedly, unexpectedly, wholeheartedly, wickedly:**
  - The weather had turned **unexpectedly** stormy.

C

Some adverbs have two forms, one ending -ly and the other not. We can sometimes use either of the two forms of the adverb without changing the meaning, although the form ending in -ly is more usual in a formal style:
  - I'll be there as **quick(ly)** as I can.   • Try to sing **loud(ly)** in the last verse.

Other words like this include **cheap(ly), clean(ly), clear(ly), fine(ly), slow(ly), thin(ly).**

D

In other cases there is a difference in the meaning of the adverb with and without -ly:
  - She gave her time **free.** (= for no money)   *and*   She gave her time **freely.** (= willingly)
  - I arrived **late** for the concert.   *and*   I haven't seen John **lately.** (= recently)

Here are some other pairs of adverbs that can have different meanings. Compare:

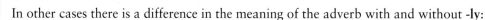

• Do I have to change trains in Leeds?' 'No, you can go **direct** (= without stopping).'	• I'll be with you **directly** (= very soon). • He saw Susan **directly** (= straight) ahead.
• She worked really **hard** and passed her exams.	• The telephone line was so bad, I could **hardly** (= only just) hear what he was saying.
• He kicked the ball **high** over the goal.	• Everyone thinks **highly** of her teaching. (= they praise her for it)
• They cut **short** their holiday when John became ill. (= went home early)	• The speaker will be arriving **shortly** (= soon). Please take your seats.
• The door was **wide** (= completely) open so I just went straight in.	• It won't be difficult to get the book. It's **widely** available. (= in many places)

E

Remember that **good** is an adjective and **well** is an adverb:
  - I asked Francis to clean the car, and he did a **good** job. / ...and he did the job **well.**

However, **well** is also an adjective meaning 'healthy':
  - You're not looking too **well.** Are you okay?

Use the rules in the extracts to correct **five** of the sentences below. Say which sections in the grammar book helped you to decide. (Only five of the sentences contain mistakes.)

1 She walked quickly to her car.

2 He played excellent.

3 I saw her dance lively.

4 He introduced her to a friendly man.

5 Is that film any good?

6 Open the window widely, please.

7 I bought my last car really cheap.

8 It was an enormous boring lecture.

9 The office was unusually noisy.

10 He waved his arms around agitatedly.

11.7 Listening

a Look at the following list of collocations to do with towns and cities. Check the meanings with your teacher or a dictionary. Then put them into one of these three categories.

1 common in towns in my country

2 rare in towns in my country

3 unheard of in towns in my country

pedestrian precinct	ring road
traffic lights	bus station
multi-storey car park	traffic jams
information centre	bypasses
pedestrian underpasses	superstore
housing estates	sports centre
swimming pool	traffic calming
shopping centre	public library
leisure facilities	shopping malls
community groups	leisure centres
video hire shops	souvenir shops
tower blocks	

b Can you think of any other phrases to do with towns and cities that use any of the words here? For example, are there other kinds of *stations*? Make a list of about twelve.

c Read the following questions, then listen to the radio interview and answer the questions.

1 How many cities did the survey cover?

2 How long did it take?

3 What's the difference between this report and ones which have come out previously?

4 What was the idea suggested in 1963 that was never taken up?

5 What has the effect of ring roads been?

6 Why is the ring road in Northampton particularly dangerous?

7 What is 'mad' about the people who go to the gym or swimming pool?

8 What categories of people find shopping a nightmare?

9 What percentage of housewives have access to a car during the week?

10 How do the politicians travel? What is the implication of this?

11.8 Writing – problem, solution, evaluation

a Put the following jumbled text in order, and decide which linking phrases helped you do so. Begin with sentence 9.

b Divide the completed text into three paragraphs. What is the topic of each paragraph?

1 One answer to both these problems is to construct specially designated bicycle paths across and through the city.

2 The main reason for this is that the parents consider the roads to be too dangerous for their children, and prefer to take them by car.

3 The advantages of such a scheme are obvious: fewer early morning traffic queues with worried parents transporting little Johnny to school; a fitter and healthier population, with resulting reductions in medical bills; a generally more positive attitude to cycling itself.

4 These differ from the existing cycle paths (which are often no more than lines painted on the sides of the roads, or sometimes on the pavements next to the roads), in that they are either some distance from the roads, or are sheltered from them by, for example, hedges or specially constructed 'islands'.

5 A bargain, I'd say.

6 This causes two separate problems: firstly, the roads themselves become jammed up with traffic which is almost entirely unnecessary; and secondly, the lack of exercise brings about a decline in children's physical fitness.

7 And what is more, the cost is, relatively speaking, low: a mile of six-lane motorway costs approximately £115 million to build: a mile of cycle path just £16,000.

8 In this way, there is no chance that either the cyclist will stray into the congested carriageway; or that the cars and lorries could encroach, perhaps dangerously, on the cyclists' space.

9 It is a strange fact that, although 96% of children between six and thirteen own a bicycle, only 4% of them use it to get to school.

One answer to the question above might be:

Paragraph 1:	Problem
Paragraph 2:	Solution
Paragraph 3:	Evaluation

This three-phase structure is a very common one in texts in English.

C Write three paragraphs which begin as suggested below. Try to use some of the linking phrases from the article which helped you in part a.

1 The biggest problem facing my country is…

2 In my opinion, the most effective solution to this problem would be to…

3 This would have several advantages: firstly…

11.9 Review

Complete the crossword.
All the words and phrases come from Unit 10.

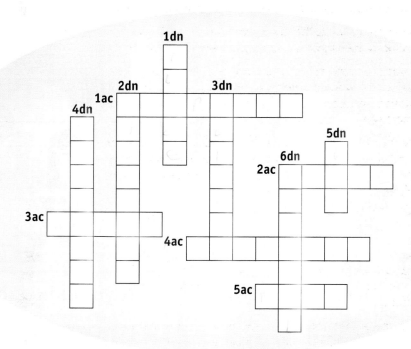

CLUES

Across (ac)

1 Very hungry. (8)

2 Follow. (5)

3 The official word for a person who is young. (5)

4 An adjective meaning not used or lived in, and falling into decay and ruin. (8)

5 A slang word which means to steal. (4)

Down (dn)

1 Another word for a big or dangerous fire. (5)

2 Go out secretly and quietly. (5,3)

3 A general word for something with wheels like a car. (7)

4 Young person who steals a car and goes for a ride. (8)

5 A slang or dialect word for boy. (3)

6 A newspaper which specialises in gossip and scandal. (7)

12

Art for art's sake?

To start you thinking

First take a few minutes to answer these questions for yourself. Then discuss your answers in groups. Find out about other people's ideas and opinions.

1 What is art – just paintings and drawings or something more?

2 Have you got a favourite artist or work of art? Why? Why not?

3 Have you ever visited an art gallery? What did you see? Did you enjoy it?

4 Which is the most famous picture in the world?

5 Are you an artist in any way?

6 Can art be 'good for you'?

7 What do you think of the art shown on this page?

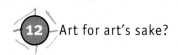
12.2 Reading

a Read through paragraphs (a–h) below and put them into the correct order. Then fill in the gaps with the words given in the box. You may use an English-English dictionary to help you. Begin with paragraph c.

> met   launched   prescribed   pilot
> level   eligible   well-being   chronic
> tackle   deprived   panic   huge
> problems   low   social   condition

MENTAL HEALTH PATIENTS to be treated with ART

(a) Like any other NHS medical treatment, the art classes will be free. Annual costs of £10,000 will be [*met*] jointly by Stockport Health Authority and the local council.

(b) 'You can give her a dose of Prozac and hope she'll get better, but you are never going to solve the problem unless you [*tackle*] how she deals with her life.' The severely disturbed and suicidal will not be [*eligible*] for the classes, to be taught by artists with no medical training in local church halls and social clubs.

1 **(c)** Patients with mental health problems are to be [*prescribed*] painting, sculpting and creative writing on the NHS, instead of drugs. 'Arts On Prescription', a radical new scheme [*launch*] this week, will enable doctors to treat depression and anxiety by sending [*chronic*] sufferers to art classes.

(d) 'Arts On Prescription' was inspired by an earlier Manchester project, 'Exercise On Prescription', where GPs prescribed free sessions in the gym or the swimming pool to patients with coronary [*problems*]. Participants reported that the greatest improvements had been to mental rather than physical [*well-being*] and demand grew for arts-based activities.

(e) A [*pilot*] scheme is to begin in various economically [*deprived*] areas of Manchester. Participating GPs, consultants, community psychiatric nurses and [*social*] workers will refer patients who suffer from mental health complaints like [*panic*] attacks to an Arts and Mental Health Nurse. The patients will then be offered a range of art classes, from drama and dance to ceramics and photography, and, after consultation, be prescribed a ten-week course.

(f) 'People find these sorts of expressive activities, done in a group, give them a chance to develop their confidence and self-esteem, and give them a social contact at a [*level*] they are comfortable with,' a community health team spokeswoman said.

(g) Schizophrenics and manic depressives in a stable [*condi*] may take part, though.

(h) 'Mental ill-health is a [*huge*] burden on the NHS, and shows itself through many physical and mental problems. This treatment gets us out of looking at everything from a problem-based viewpoint.' A typical patient, she said, would be a woman with a family and little time to herself, struggling with relationship difficulties and suffering [*low*] self-esteem, insomnia and lack of motivation.

C D F H B G F A

b Decide if the following statements are true or false.

1 Mental health patients will not be offered music classes.

2 Doctors will run the arts classes.

3 This type of treatment is intended to prevent further illness.

4 This scheme is to be introduced all over Manchester.

5 This type of treatment must be paid for by each patient.

6 The previous project 'Exercise On Prescription' provided great physical improvements for sufferers.

7 Certain mental health patients will not be offered this treatment.

8 The mental health team spokeswoman thinks drugs like Prozac soon make people better.

9 Each ten-week course of treatment will cost £10,000.

10 The courses will not take place in hospitals.

12.3 Reading

Read the following questions, then scan through the advertisements for art shows and answer the questions.

1 Which show is currently touring the country?

2 How many of the exhibitions are in Edinburgh?

3 Which artist's work doesn't the critic like?

4 Which artist uses a type of collage?

5 Which artist sometimes used criminals as his subjects?

6 Which artist's work has been ignored for too long, according to the critic?

7 In the critic's opinion, which show should have included more artists?

8 Who were Winslow Homer and J.S. Sargent?

9 What's the name of the recently re-discovered great British Modernist painter?

10 Which show encourages young artists?

11 Which artist takes photographs of buildings being destroyed?

12 Which show is going on for the longest time?

13 Which artists produce abstract art?

14 How many of the shows end today?

15 Which show is definitely exhibiting some forms of sculpture?

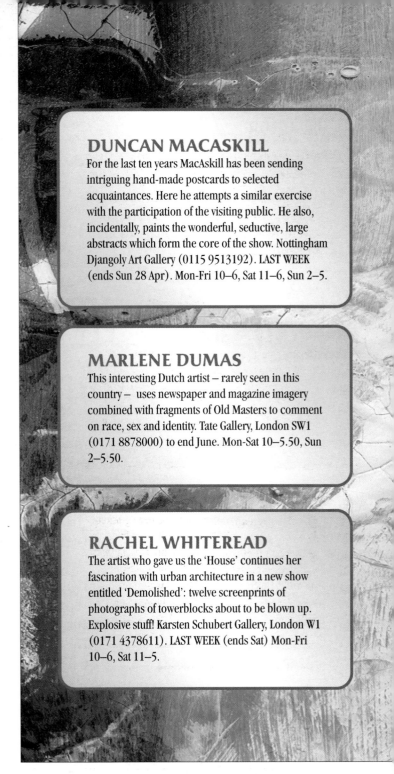

DUNCAN MACASKILL
For the last ten years MacAskill has been sending intriguing hand-made postcards to selected acquaintances. Here he attempts a similar exercise with the participation of the visiting public. He also, incidentally, paints the wonderful, seductive, large abstracts which form the core of the show. Nottingham Djangoly Art Gallery (0115 9513192). LAST WEEK (ends Sun 28 Apr). Mon-Fri 10–6, Sat 11–6, Sun 2–5.

MARLENE DUMAS
This interesting Dutch artist – rarely seen in this country – uses newspaper and magazine imagery combined with fragments of Old Masters to comment on race, sex and identity. Tate Gallery, London SW1 (0171 8878000) to end June. Mon-Sat 10–5.50, Sun 2–5.50.

RACHEL WHITEREAD
The artist who gave us the 'House' continues her fascination with urban architecture in a new show entitled 'Demolished': twelve screenprints of photographs of towerblocks about to be blown up. Explosive stuff! Karsten Schubert Gallery, London W1 (0171 4378611). LAST WEEK (ends Sat) Mon-Fri 10–6, Sat 11–5.

JOHN DEAKIN

This full-scale retrospective of the remarkable photographer includes moody and bohemian portraits of Soho characters – artists, film stars, poets, criminals – in the 50s and 60s. Plus the shots Deakin took as a *Vogue* staffer. National Portrait Gallery, London WC2 (0171 3060055) to 14 July. Mon-Sat 10–6, Sun 12–6.

FREDERIC LEIGHTON

The Royal Academy celebrates its former president. Not much fun but all you need to know about Leighton's academic, classical and basically phoney art. Royal Academy, London W1 (0171 4397438). ENDS TODAY. 10–6.

JASPER JOHNS

Seductive and witty sculptures by the distinguished American Pop artist and guru. A coffee pot filled with paint brushes, beer cans and bronze lightbulbs challenge our perceptions of illusion and reality, art and the everyday. Leeds City Art Gallery (01132 478248) to 2 Jun. Mon & Tues, Thurs-Sat 10–5, Wed 10–8, Sun 1–5.

BRITISH FOLK ART

Privately rescued from dispersal after it was turned out of its old home in Bath, the peerless British Folk Art Collection is currently on a continuous tour of the country. Engagingly naive images and artefacts, ranging from pictures of pigs to painted signs for shop doorways and a tray by the great Modernist discovery, Alfred Wallis. Eastbourne Towner Art Gallery (01323 417961). ENDS TODAY. 2–5.

JACK YEATS

Yeats, brother of the more famous W.B., created works of art that are unmistakably Irish and utterly idiosyncratic. Here is a small glimpse of the paintings for which Samuel Beckett called Yeats 'a supreme master'. Bright, primary landscapes and the people who inhabited them by a no-longer neglected visionary. Manchester City Art Gallery (0161 2365244). ENDS TOMORROW. 2–5.30.

AWASH IN COLOUR:
Great American watercolours from the Museum of Fine Arts, Boston

In an inspired move, the National Galleries of Scotland have borrowed a superb collection of watercolours. This well-chosen group, including fine examples of the work of Winslow Homer and J.S. Sargent and a curious early Edward Hopper, charts the achievement of the American watercolourist during the late 19th and early 20th centuries and points the way towards the explosion of Modernism. Edinburgh NGoS (0131 5568921) to 14 Jul. Mon-Sat 10–5, Sun 2–5.

MARK ROTHKO

It seems an inspired and brave idea for the Tate St. Ives to hang a few of the National Collection's many Rothkos alongside works by the St. Ives abstractionists. But why leave it at that? What is needed is a full comparison of the New York and Cornish artists of the period, and in particular Heron and Louis and de Kooning and Lanyon. Tate St. Ives (01736 796226) to 3 Nov. Mon-Sat 11–7, Sun 11–5.

ROYAL SCOTTISH ACADEMY

The annual outing for Scotland's art establishment, always enjoyable, is made more so this year by extending the invitation to exhibit to young unknowns. The evidence is that Scotland's creative originality is as strong as ever. Edinburgh Royal Scottish Academy (0131 2256671) to 6 Jul. Mon-Sat 10–5, Sun 2–5.

(12.4) Vocabulary

a Put the words in the list below in the best place on the brain map. Some words may be in more than one place! Then add some of your own words.

> watercolours marble oils landscape wood brush abstract fresco easel
> portrait model negatives frame shot chisel sketch palette surrealism
> canvas close-up hammer impressionism perspective exposure bust
> charcoal collage still life

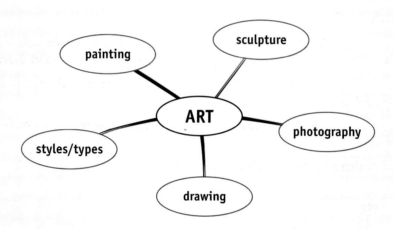

b Now complete the following sentences with appropriate vocabulary from the brain map.

1 The manor house is full of beautifully painted .... of the family's ancestors.

2 Ageing film stars often refuse to have .... shots taken, for obvious reasons!

3 Her best work was done using simple .... on paper.

4 There was a marble .... of Mozart on his desk.

5 It wasn't until the 15th century that artists rediscovered the rules of ....

6 .... attempts to show the world of dreams and subconscious thought.

7 Some artists insist that the .... is just as important as the painting it surrounds.

8 If it's dark, you'll need a very slow ...., unless you use a flash of course.

9 I find .... rather boring – just shiny food and drink on a table, isn't it?

10 Julio did only a very quick .... but it looked just like me!

12.5 Grammar – future forms

a Look at these examples from reading texts 12.2 and 12.3, and choose the descriptions of use and grammar names for each example.

Examples		Use	Name
12.2	…the art classes will be free.	*c*	*Future Simple*
	A pilot scheme is to begin …		
	Patients … are to be prescribed painting, …		
12.3	LAST WEEK (ends Sun 28 Apr).		
	… towerblocks [which are] about to be blown up.		

Descriptions of use

a Used in formal style for plans and arrangements usually when they are official. Very much more common in written English. (Two other uses are giving orders and describing destiny.)

b Used when talking about events in the future which are determined by a timetable or something similar.

c Has many uses, but used here as the 'Pure Future' simply to state future events. More common in written style.

d Used to show that a future event is very close indeed.

Grammar names:

be about to + infinitive   be + infinitive   Future Simple   Present Simple

b Complete the following sentences with the most suitable future form from this unit and Unit 2. If there is more than one possible answer, think how this may change the meaning.

1 What .... you .... (do) after you .... (leave) art school next year?

2 Just think, this time next week you .... (exhibit) your sculptures in New York!

3 Sorry I can't come to the opening of your exhibition on Saturday but I .... (have) dinner with some old friends from university.

4 My Arts of the Renaissance course .... (start) tomorrow and I'm really excited.

5 All the major galleries in the London area have been notified that the director of the Arts Council .... (visit) them next month.

6 By this time next year, we .... (graduate) as professional art therapists.

7 Help, this vase is too heavy – I .... (drop) it!

8 And now *Popular Arts Live* is proud to welcome this week's special guest who .... (demonstrate) her special technique on TV for the very first time!

12.6 Writing – revising and editing written work

Revising is the most important stage of the writing process. It involves checking that the content and purpose are both clear and appropriate to the situation and intended reader. As well as checking spelling, punctuation and grammar, it also involves adding or leaving out words, rearranging and changing.

Here is a review of an art show written for the local newspaper. Make any changes you think are necessary.

WILL AUDREY MAKE YOU LOSE YOUR SENSES

Audrey Walker's new 'experience art room' show is really good. Audrey Walker is in fact a local girl who has developed the style she has now over several years. While she was living in Tokyo.

The show take place inside one large dark room. The room has no windows. She describes the show as 'a sensory adventure' and as you enter into the room you find out why she describes it like that!

The first sense to be afected is smell. Inside the room there is a dim blue light but little else is visible. Suddenly then you are hit by strange aromas – oranges, ammonia, mown grass, tar, aftershave, burning rubber, roses, wet dog, etc.

Next it comes sound. But the sounds don't immediately correspond the smells. The smells don't go away. So you might get birdsong with burning rubber, traffic noise with aftershave, a chainsaw with oranges.

She says this is where does the true aventure start, you have to make your own connections. And you do start make your own absolutely wierd connections.

Then, still in the same blue light, you walk around and touch things. The things dramatically are illuminated and draw you to them. She calls this the 'feelie part'. You might touch a tree trunk, while listening to a dentists drill and smelling a strong cheese!

The final stage is eyes. This is achieved with holgrams. The holograms are very convincing and appear in the middle of the room because you can walk around them and get a 3–D effect. Your senses are bombarded with controdictions. One I still remember is seeing a spinning sheeps head, while touching a pineapple, hearing whale's singing and smelling vinegar!

The show is for the next two weeks at the Modern Art Gallery in Bristol Street. It will drive you out your senses. Don't miss it!

12.7 Listening

Read these notes made by a student during a seminar about Michelangelo Buonarroti. Then listen to part of the seminar and make corrections to the notes.

1   Michelangelo Buonarroti (1465—1564).
2   45 years younger than Leonardo da Vinci.
3   'Cinquecento' = 15th century (1400—1499).
4   Worked for Domenico Ghirlandajo for 13 years.
5   Studied anatomy — drew dead bodies! Ugh!
6   Leonardo only interested in human body — Michelangelo much more wide-ranging.
7   By 30, Michelangelo considered greater genius than Leonardo.
8   Probably greatest work = wall of Sistine Chapel.
9   Michelangelo worked alone for 5 years to complete Sistine Chapel fresco.
10 Most famous detail = 'Decoration of Adam'.

12.8 Hearing perception

Follow the instructions given by your teacher.

12.9 Pronunciation – unstressed endings

One-syllable words containing **-age** are pronounced / eɪdʒ / but this is generally not true for polysyllabic words.

Examples:

GROUP 1	GROUP 2	GROUP 3
One-syllable words (always /eɪdʒ/)	Polysyllabic words (generally /ɪdʒ/)	Polysyllabic words (sometimes /aːʒ/)
page	encourage	camouflage

a Put the following words in the correct group. Use an English-English dictionary if you are not sure!

cottage   stage   marriage   rage
courage   massage   cabbage   image
collage   language   garage   savage
sausage   barrage   carriage   heritage
wage   dressage   bandage   postage

b Now listen to the quiz questions. When you hear the tone, say your answer. CLUE – all the answers finish with –age!

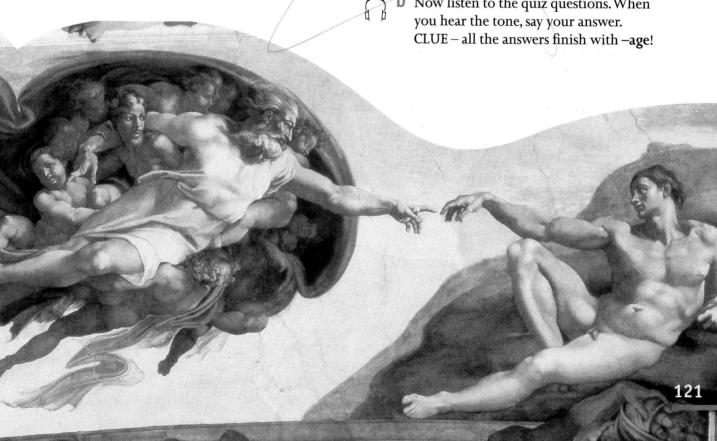

c One-syllable words with **–ace** are pronounced /eɪs/ (e.g. face) but in polysyllabic words it usually changes to /ɪs/ (e.g. surface /sɜːfɪs/) or /əs/ (e.g. grimace /grɪməs/).

One-syllable words with **–ate** are pronounced /eɪt/ (e.g. rate) but in polysyllabic **nouns** and **adjectives** it generally changes to /ət/ (e.g. elaborate /ɪlæbərət/). This does **not** happen with **verbs**, which retain the /eɪt/ pronunciation (e.g. hesitate /hezɪteɪt/).

In pairs, read through the following sentences and decide how **–ace** and **–ate** are pronounced in the words in **bold** and note down the correct pronunciation using the phonetic script shown above.

1 Can you give me an **estimate** of how much it's worth?

Sorry, madam, it's impossible to **estimate** something like that until I've seen the piece.

2 He was so **desperate** to pass the exam that he forged the **certificate**.

3 Certain rooms in the **palace** are open to the public but most of them are **private**.

4 **Climate** change is going to become a greater **menace** over the next fifty years.

5 We sat out on the **terrace** drinking hot **chocolate**.

6 Susan won't **tolerate** anything less than **immaculate** clothing for her children.

7 The **preface** to the book didn't give a very **accurate** description of the real situation.

8 June was told to report the theft of her **necklace** to the **consulate**.

9 Let's **separate** the different vegetables and put them into **separate** pans.

10 There was a **deliberate** attempt to blow up the **Senate** building at **approximately** 11 p.m. yesterday.

d Now listen to the recording, check your answers and practise saying the sentences.

12.10 **Review**

The collocations in **bold** below, which all come from Unit 11, have something wrong with them. Correct the wrong words.

1 It's advisable to have a good **socialist mix** in any company.

2 Most people prefer to buy things in **shopping mills** nowadays.

3 The report concluded that many **inside city** schools were overcrowded and underfunded.

4 Most factories are cutting their **labour field** and replacing them with machines controlled by computers.

5 There have been far fewer accidents in the city since the **round road** was completed.

6 The council are going to put ramps in the road as part of their **traffic cooling** campaign.

7 There has been a price war between the big do-it-yourself **supershops**.

8 Many of the **tower buildings** built in the 1960s have had to be demolished as they were so badly constructed.

9 You can't drive through the city centre any more – it's been turned into a **pedestrian precept**.

10 The new **mega-storey car park** was the ugliest building imaginable.

LIST B

○ ○	○ ○ ○ ○
pilot	reproduces
○ ○ ○	○ ○ ○
literature	character
○ ○ ○○	○ ○
associates	devise
○ ○ ○	○ ○
regarded	jigsaw
○ ○	○ ○ ○
excused	enjoyment

What a good idea!

(13.1) To start you thinking

Discuss these questions in pairs or small groups.

1   Which single gadget or device would you take to a desert island?

2   What do you think is the most useful or important invention of the twentieth century?

3   Why do people always try to make new technological developments?

4   Can you think of an example of a recent technological development which you think is a bad thing for the human race?

(13.2) Reading

a   You are going to read a newspaper article describing the history of an everyday object which is so common that you use the brand name to mean the object itself. Before you read, try to guess the answers to the following questions:

1   What is the object?

2   What is the brand name?

3   Why does it have this name?

4   When (approximately) was the object invented?

5   Why did the inventor receive no money from this invention?

b   Now read the article quickly and check your answers.

The secret is not putting too fine a point on it

It's 50 years since the Biro hit Britain and put an end to blots, blotches and inkpots. Jonathan Sale pens a brief tribute.

The Biro hit the shops of Britain 50 years ago. In the run-up to Christmas 1945, this was no *el cheapo* chuckaway item costing a few pence but a luxury purchase. At 55 shillings (£2.75) it cost the weekly wage of a secretary. Yet within four years the new writing device was outselling old-fashioned fountain pens.

The launch of a rival ballpoint pen in the United States at the end of October 1945 had been equally spectacular. Despite the dubious advertising campaign promising 'the first pen that writes under water', the New York store Gimbel's shifted almost 10,000 at $12.50 each. Notes to the milkman, and handwriting, would never be the same.

Strictly speaking, the ballpoint is not 50 years old, but 100 – a primitive version dates back to 1895. Nothing came of this, nor of later patents of different designs that used ordinary ink stored in a pad stuffed down the barrel. The breakthrough came in 1938 when Laszlo Biro, Hungarian journalist, hypnotist and sculptor, was visiting the Budapest printers of an arts magazine which he edited. It dawned on him that a pen would be much more useful if its ink dried as quickly as his page proofs. Using ink that resembled runny jelly, he developed and patented the workable prototype of a blot-free pen.

Escaping to Paris from the German invasion, he became friendly with the President of Argentina, who invited him to develop his invention in Buenos Aires. Here Laszlo approached Henry Martin, a businessman visiting the area on British government business, who was intrigued by the idea that a Biro, unlike a fountain pen, is unaffected by changes in air pressure. Martin was aware that navigators in bombers were suffering from ink splodges all over their calculations and set in train the manufacture of ballpoints both in Argentina and, together with the Miles Aircraft Company, in Britain.

The Biro became a crucial part of the British war effort. The Miles-Martin Pen Company turned a disused aircraft hangar near Reading into a Biro factory in which 20 young women banged out 30,000 ballpoints so that RAF staff could write for victory.

Meanwhile, back in Buenos Aires, the first Biros were being sold, retailing at the equivalent of £25. Unfortunately, Laszlo had not got around to registering the patent in the US and so received no royalties from the massive sales at Gimbel's and other stores. He concentrated instead on his art: he also tried out a few other inventions, none of which had the ballpoint's success.

The ballpoint also made a household name of another entrepreneur. Baron Michel Bich was a French plastics manufacturer who had, like Laszlo, a flash of inspiration. He made plastic components for pen manufacturers. While delivering a pile of disparate parts in the early fifties, it occurred to him that he could come up with something a great deal simpler.

The result was the disposable Bic (the 'h' was dropped to avoid any embarrassing confusion with 'bitch') Crystal, launched in France in 1953. It is now the brand leader, retailing at about 18p. The theory is that you could draw a line more than 1.5 miles long before the ink, made to a secret, solvent-based formula, ran out.

Worldwide, 15 million Bic Crystals are sold every day, around half of the total of all ballpoints. In 1957 the French company took over the British competition but Laszlo lives on in the Biro Minor. When Baron Bich died in May 1994, he was the fifth-richest man in France.

But, calligraphically speaking, did Messrs Biro and Bich do our fingers a favour? Or did they leave us with a legacy of junk handwriting? My own ballpoint poised, I turned to Humphrey Lyttleton, president of the Society for Italic Handwriting, who produces as attractive a note on paper as he does from his trumpet. Would we be better off without ballpoints?

'The people who say that they make them scrawl are absolutely right. It is hard to do your nicest handwriting. It is comparable to doing figure-skating on ice with roller-skates. It gives a feeling of insecurity. You can't get that lovely even movement with uprights parallel to each other; they lean to the back or front.'

But he does not write off ballpoints. 'There is no doubt that they flow evenly and don't make holes in the paper. In fact, I say that it's a jolly good invention. It has the advantages of speed and guaranteed even flow – and with a calligraphy pen, you can't write letters in the bath.'

c Put these events in the story of the ballpoint into the correct order, and date roughly each development. The article was written in 1996.

1 Biro meets Henry Martin

2 Launch of Biro in Britain

3 Bic took over their British rivals

4 Laszlo Biro has idea about a blot-free pen

5 Baron Bich has idea for simplifying plastic pen parts

6 Launch of rival ballpoint in US

7 Biro escapes to Paris

8 Biros start to sell more than fountain pens

9 Primitive version of the ballpoint first invented

10 First Biro factory opens in Britain

d Answer the following questions.

1 What do you think *el cheapo* (line 3) means?

2 Was the biro always inexpensive?

3 Where was the ink stored in the earliest ballpoints?

4 What did Laszlo Biro realise in 1938?

5 Why was Henry Martin so interested in the pen?

6 What proportion of ballpoints sold are Bics?

7 Do ballpoints improve people's handwriting?

8 Is Humphrey Lyttleton's opinion of ballpoints entirely negative?

13.3 Vocabulary

a Look at the following list of multi-word verbs from the article. By working out what they mean from the context, match the verbs with the definitions underneath. Do not use a dictionary.

date back (line 18)   dawn on (line 25)

turn into (line 42)   bang out (line 44)

get around to (line 48)   try out (line 51)

come up with (line 59)   run out (line 66)

take over (line 69)   turn to (line 77)

write off (line 90)

1 test something by using it

2 consider as useless or a failure

3 change in form or nature

4 be invented in, exist since

5 go to for help or advice

6 gain control over

7 become obvious to

8 think of, invent

9 do at last

10 produce, make

11 come to an end, be used up

b Practise using the verbs above by discussing the following questions in small groups.

1 Who do you turn to when you have a problem? Why?

2 When do your English studies date back to? Why did you start studying English?

3 Is there some new learning technique you would like to try out? What? Why?

4 Do you think the world will ever run out of petrol? When?

5 Is there anything you should have got round to recently, but haven't? Do you feel guilty about it?

6 Do you think anybody will ever come up with a computer that is more intelligent than a human?

7 Has anybody ever written you off? When? Why? How did you feel about it?

8 When does a boy turn into a man?

9 When did it dawn on you that English was a useful language to learn?

10 Do you think a lot about your English homework, or do you just bang it out?

11 If you had the opportunity to take over your school, what changes would you make?

(13.4) Grammar – multi-word verbs

a Multi-word verbs are verbs which have two or three parts: a main verb (like *look, put* or *bring*) and one or two particles (like *up, down* or *through*). Look at these examples from the passage about the Biro in 13.2, and underline the multi-word verbs.

1 … before the ink ran out. (line 66)

2 It dawned on him that … (line 25)

3 [They] turned a disused aircraft hangar near Reading into a Biro factory … (line 42)

4 … he also tried out a few other inventions … (line 51)

5 … he could come up with something a great deal simpler. (line 59)

b The following sentences all contain verbs from 13.3, but some of them have been used wrongly. Find the sentences that are wrong and correct them.

1 We won't know if the idea will work until we try out it.

2 It was important to produce as many uniforms as possible, and at one point we were banging out them at the rate of 10,000 a day.

3 This machine dates back to 1765.

4 I want you to come up with a good idea, Bart, and I want you to come up it with NOW!

5 I can always turn the production manager to if there are any problems.

6 Companies know the importance of investing in research and development, but many only get round to it when their sales figures start to drop.

7 When I examined the manufacturing process it dawned me on that we could make the product much more cheaply.

8 Don't write Nancy off; she's an excellent designer.

9 Natural resources are running out and we'll have to change our way of life in order to survive.

10 The alchemists were ancient scientists who searched for a way to turn ordinary metals into gold.

11 The *Prestige Pen Company* is so weak that someone is sure to try and take it over soon.

c Look at the verbs in part b again. Which category does each verb belong to?

CATEGORY
1 Verbs which have no object – *intransitive verbs*.
2 Multi-word verbs whose main verb and particle are never separated by the object – *indivisible verbs*.
3 Multi-word verbs whose main verb and particle(s) can be separated by the object – *divisible verbs*. • If the object is a noun, you can put it before or after the particle. • If the object is a pronoun, you must put it between the main verb and the particle.
4 Multi-word verbs which have more than one particle. These are generally *indivisible*.

d Your dictionary should tell you which type each verb is. Find the following verbs in your dictionary, decide which type they are and write the correct category number from the table after each verb.

1 put up (= have someone stay in your house) ...*type 3*...

2 look out (= be careful)

3 go down with (= become ill with an infection or disease)

4 put on (= start wearing a piece of clothing)

5 go through (= check carefully)

6 take after (= look or act like your mother or father)

7 set off (= leave to start a journey or trip)

8 get to (= arrive somewhere)

9 call off (= cancel)

10 take out (= remove)

e Now use the verbs from part d to complete these sentences. If the sentence has an object in brackets, put it in the correct place with the verb.

1 Mr Ishida is coming over from Japan for a few days to check our computer system, and I've offered to .... for a few days. (him)

2 That equipment is really old so you'd better ....

3 There's a new flu around, and so many staff have .... that production has almost stopped. (it)

4 If we're going to use that acid, I'll just .... (my goggles)

5 I don't understand your diagrams. Can we just .... again. (them)

6 She .... (her father) He was an inventor too – just like her.

7 Explorers in the Antarctic never .... on a journey without a satellite navigation system.

8 In twenty years, aircraft will be so fast that you'll be able to .... in a few hours. (the other side of the world)

9 The road trials on the new motorcycle design should have been yesterday, but the weather was so bad that we had to .... (them)

10 The new technician objected to several parts of his contract and refused to sign it until the management had .... (them)

(13.5) Pronunciation – nouns from multi-word verbs

Many multi-word verbs can be made into nouns.

Examples:

break down (v) – The car broke down on the way to the airport.
break-down (n) – We had a break-down on the way to the airport.

take off (v) – The plane took off about twenty minutes late.
take-off (n) – The times of maximum stress for a pilot are take-off and landing.

However, the pronunciation is different – in particular the stress.

 a Listen to the sentences above and mark the stress. Can you see any pattern that helps you form a rule?

b Now look at these sentences and say whether the stress will be on the verb (*check, back, go* etc.) or on the particle (*in, up, ahead* etc.). Mark the stress with a bubble: the first two have been done as an example.

1 You have to check ⓞin at least two hours before the flight.

2 There's an automatic back-ⓞup every thirty minutes.

3 The new model has been given the go-ahead.

4 The school is trying to build up a library of CD-ROM material.

5 The fumes were so strong that he blacked out for a few seconds.

6 The accident is a real setback for the US space programme.

7 We decided to print out the document.

8 The company has decided to go ahead with the new project.

9 There was a total black-out all over New York.

10 The pay-out in this week's lottery is £12 million.

11 The computer print-out for the program was over twenty pages.

12 The bad weather will set back our building plans.

13 It is imperative to back up at least once a day.

14 We've discovered a dangerous build-up of gases in the pipes.

15 The new cashpoint machines will only pay out if they recognise your thumbprint.

c Now listen to the tape and decide if you were right.

d Listen to the tape again and practise the stress.

13.6 Collocations

Look at the following collocations from the article in 13.2. Decide what they mean, and write one in each of the spaces below.

luxury purchase (line 4)
weekly wage (line 5)
advertising campaign (line 12)
on business (line 34)
register a patent (line 48)
massive sales (line 49)
household name (line 53)
brand leader (line 63)
secret formula (line 65)

1 Everybody knows that Coca-Cola is made to a .... , but nobody knows what it is!

2 The average .... of workers in Britain has risen steadily since the war.

3 She's gone to France ....

4 You would expect Merlet to be popular in his own country – but in fact his book has had .... in every country except France.

5 The product is well-known, but it's hardly a ....

6 Things like CD players and TVs used to be a ...., but now everybody's got them.

7 Nowadays, it seems that any .... will use sex to sell the product.

8 If you invent something, it's a good idea to .... for it the next day!

9 It's the ultimate aim of every company to make their product the ....

13.7 Writing – improving your style

The writer George Orwell produced the following simple list of six ideas for improving your written English style.

1 Never use a metaphor, simile or other figure of speech which you are used to seeing in print.

2 Never use a long word where a short word will do.

3 If it is possible to cut a word out, always cut it out.

4 Never use the passive where you can use the active.

5 Never use a foreign phrase, a scientific word or a jargon word if you can think of an everyday English equivalent.

6 Break any of these rules sooner than say anything outright barbarous.

Read this passage about a famous 'good idea'. Using Orwell's rules, change the piece to make it easier to read.

13.8 Listening

a Discuss with a partner which of these two calculators you would buy, if you had the money, and why.

Modern machines and gadgets are extremely complicated. Why do you think people like to buy complicated things?

It is a fact that is well-known by all English schoolchildren that the *sandwich* is named after the Earl of Sandwich, a British aristocrat and noble gentleman of the eighteenth century. This aforementioned Earl was one evening playing at cards, as was often and frequently his habitual routine, when he was suddenly, and without any warning, attacked by hunger. Since he had no intention – or, indeed, any desire – to interrupt his precious game of cards (and additionally having no wish that his playing companions should be disturbed), he demanded that the servants of the club should bring him something that he might consume.

The servant, having ascertained from the cook that there was an insufficiency of comestibles in the kitchen, reported back to the Earl that he could find only a couple of slices of bread and a piece of cold meat. 'In that case,' said the Earl, 'please would you be so kind as to place the meat between the two slices of bread, and bring it to me.'

This snack, which was in this way newly invented, became most fashionable in the sophisticated clubs and salons of eighteenth century London, was given the name *sandwich* after the Earl, and has remained popular ever since that day.

Presumably, it can be said, that if the Earl had come from Newcastle rather than from Sandwich, we would nowadays be asking for a *ham newcastle* or an *egg newcastle*. Such are the mysteries of language!

b You are going to listen to a Professor of Computing Research explaining why the manufacturers of gadgets and machines make them so complicated. First read the following questions, then listen to the interview and answer the questions.

PART 1

1 Why do travel brochures tell you different things about different hotels?

2 When you read a travel brochure, how do you usually choose a hotel, according to the Professor?

3 Why do the travel companies want people to choose hotels in this way?

4 What is the main point that the Professor is making in this part?

PART 2

5 What is a 'safety-critical system', do you think?

6 What's the difference between a video recorder and an aeroplane cockpit?

7 What does he mean when he says 'it's no longer a joke – it's deadly serious'?

8 Why are these systems so complicated, according to the Professor?

9 Why is it 'better' to blame the pilot than blame the aeroplane, when it crashes?

(13.9) Hearing perception

Follow the instructions given by your teacher.

(13.10) Learner training

The amount of time you spend in the classroom may be very small. You need to maximise your time **outside** the class as well, so as to maintain as much contact as possible with authentic English.

a Read the following flowchart, which is designed to point you towards sources of authentic English in your immediate environment. Work your way through it. There are no right answers!

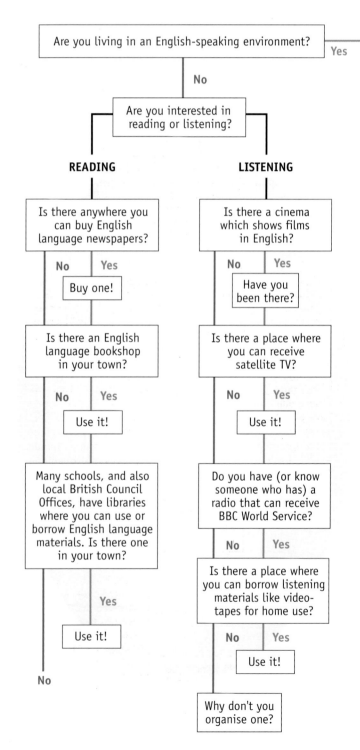

b Now go out into your immediate environment, and research the questions which are in the flowchart.

c Bring the information back to the class, and tell your classmates and teacher what you have discovered.

d Work in groups. Using the information you have gathered, present it in written form. You decide what form this text should take.

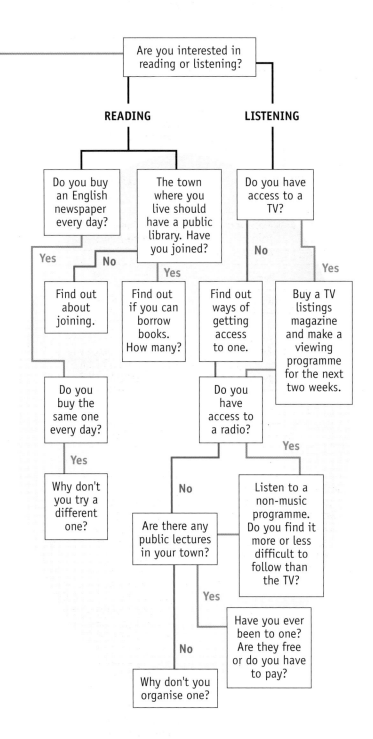

13.11 Review

The following words, from which the vowels have been removed, all appeared in Unit 12. Put back the missing vowels, and match the words with the definitions in the right-hand column. The first one has been done as an example.

1 PRSPCTV
perspective

2 CHSL

3 CNVS

4 WTRCLR

5 PNTBRSH

6 RTRSPCTV

7 CLS–P

8 FRM

9 NGTV

10 FRSC

11 RT GLLRY

12 SL

a a border, usually made of wood or metal, around a picture or painting

b a brush for spreading paint on a surface

c the way that solid objects appear to have depth and distance

d a wooden frame to support a picture while the artist is working on it

e a picture painted using colours mixed with water

f a photograph taken from very near

g a room or building where works of art are shown

h steel tool for shaping wood, stone or metal

i a photograph showing dark areas as light and light areas as dark

j painting in water colour on a surface, usually of a wall, made of wet plaster

k a show of a painter's work from the earliest years up to the present time

l strong rough cloth used for an oil painting

14

Working nine to five

Look at these factors to do with the quality of a job. Which do you think are very important, quite important, not very important or not important at all? Discuss your answers with your partner.

1 the pay

2 the hours

3 how much responsibility you have

4 your colleagues

5 how much holiday you get

6 the physical conditions of the work-place

7 how much variety there is

(14.2) Reading

a Look at the two photographs above. What do you think the two women do for a living? Explain the reasons for your ideas.

b You are going to read Laura and Susan's descriptions of their jobs. First look at the twelve extracts at the top of the following page and answer the questions.

1 What jobs do the women do?

2 Which extract refers to which job?

Lunch is 1 p.m. to 2 p.m., when I go to the canteen.

I read my e-mail ...

...life, from early morning until he finishes a business dinner in the evening.

It usually disappears before I can catch it...

Then I write out a detailed report on what I've found and offer recommendations to help the customer prevent a recurrence.

Duncan is in the office from 6.30 a.m.

When I visit a customer for the first time, I make a site-plan of their premises, labelling all the rooms and drawing up a check-list of areas to explore...

I have to decide who to allocate time to and who to delay tactfully. Sometimes I refer callers to other managers.

At the end of the day I pass all the post to Duncan, who returns it to me...

Occasionally, I'm asked to give talks...

I drive to my first job, arriving at about 8 a.m.

...technicians often ask me to identify new or strange varieties.

C Now read the two descriptions below and on the following page and check your answers.

Name:	Laura
Age:	29
Occupation:	Field Biologist for Rentokil, London N12

Route to job:
Laura left school at eighteen with A levels and took a BSc in Psychology at Reading University. Recruited by Rentokil at a graduate-recruitment fair, she became a pest-control technician, working in all kinds of premises, from private houses to food factories. Two years later, she was promoted to field biologist, a job that involved inspecting and treating pests in large food factories and retail outlets.

Dress:
Blue overalls, black safety boots and a mask and gloves during treatments. A blue hairnet and red hat when in the production areas of food factories.

Name:	Susan
Age:	31
Occupation:	Personal Assistant to Duncan Lewis, Chief Executive of Mercury Communications Ltd

Route to job:
Susan left school at sixteen and took a two-year City and Guilds in Catering at Hastings College of Further Education. She spent five years as a restaurant manager at various hotels, then at 23 went to Switzerland for a year as an au pair to improve her French. Back in England, she paid her way through a one-year bilingual secretarial course at Hastings College, then worked for two years as a secretary to the managing director of Auscot Ltd, an international fish-broking company. Four years ago, she moved to Cable & Wireless, which owns Mercury, and worked as secretary to the marketing director of a new global division. When the marketing director left two years later, she became Duncan Lewis's PA and moved to Mercury when he became Chief Executive of the company in late 1994.

Dress:
Smart business clothes.

Susan's day:

I get up at 6 a.m. and leave the house at 6.40 a.m. I catch the train to work to be at my desk at about 8.30 a.m. Duncan is in the office from 6.30 a.m., so I'm busy as soon as I get in. If he is out of the office, my position is one of great responsibility. I read my e-mail and look over Duncan's to alert him to business issues as they arise. My assistant opens the post and logs it, then I look through it and make notes. At the end of the day I pass all the post to Duncan, who returns it to me with his comments or instructions.

A large part of my work is managing his diary. The phones start ringing at 9 a.m., mostly with people wanting to see him. He has an open-door policy, so the day is full of interruptions. I have to decide who to allocate time to and who to delay tactfully. Sometimes I refer callers to other managers. I plan Duncan's diary two or three weeks ahead, arranging to have briefs for meetings sent in, organising off-site meetings, as well as overseeing his travel itineraries. Duncan trusts me completely and confides in me 100 per cent.

Lunch is 1 p.m to 2 p.m., when I go to the canteen. Once a week, Duncan has a meeting with about fifteen senior managers, and I plan the agenda and take the minutes. It keeps me up to date with what's going on in the company.

I enjoy organising Duncan's life, from early morning until he finishes a business dinner in the evening. I send out invitations, book restaurants, theatre tickets – and I invite his guests for Sunday lunch.

I leave the office at 6.30 p.m. at the latest. I get home at 8.15 p.m and switch off immediately. I sleep a lot on the train home.

Laura's day:

I get up at 6.45 a.m. and leave the house between 7 a.m. and 7.30 a.m. I drive to my first job, arriving at about 8 a.m. When I visit a customer for the first time, I make a site-plan of the premises, labelling all the rooms and drawing up a check-list of areas to explore when we do our treatments. I decide where to put 'monitors' – bait and insect traps – and then lay these out with the help of a technician.

I visit most of my regular customers on a quarterly basis and carry out in-depth inspections for all manner of pests, by checking the monitors and looking for signs of pest activity. Rats, mice and cockroaches are pretty standard, but I'm also looking for a group of insects known as 'stored-goods insects', which infests raw materials. Insect identification is a very important part of the job, and technicians often ask me to identify new or strange varieties.

If I'm visiting a regular customer, I meet up with my contacts at the site and begin a check of the premises. I try to work out if there are any pests, where they are coming from and where they are likely to be now. Then I write out a detailed report on what I've found and offer recommendations to help the customer prevent a recurrence.

If I come across a pest, I obviously deal with it on the spot. If I see a live rat or mouse, it usually disappears before I can catch it, so I lay down poison to bait it. If I find any dead rats or mice, I take them away, and if I come across cockroaches or other insects, I carry out spray treatments.

I do between one and three jobs a day. At around 1 p.m. I'll grab a sandwich and eat it in the car or have something in the canteen of the site I'm visiting. Most of the time I work alone and it can get lonely, but every now and then I go on refresher and update courses, or help to train new recruits. Occasionally I'm asked to give talks on pest control.

I usually finish work at around 5 p.m. and switch off as soon as I get home.

d True or false? You should use a dictionary for this section.

1 Laura spent two years as a pest-control technician.

2 She always wears protection for her hair.

3 When she visits a new customer, she explores all parts of the building.

4 She visits her regular customers every three months.

5 The commonest pests are rats, mice and cockroaches.

6 'Stored-goods insects' would probably be found inside the walls of the building.

7 If Laura finds a pest, she does something about it immediately.

8 She deals with live rats by poisoning them.

9 She has a long lunch.

10 Her refresher courses are not very frequent.

11 She thinks about her job a lot outside work.

12 Susan was a restaurant manager by the time she was 22.

13 She got a grant to do the secretarial course.

14 She reads her boss's e-mail so that he won't be surprised by its contents.

15 Three different people deal with his post.

16 Anybody who wants to see Duncan gets to see him.

17 Duncan tells her everything.

14.3 Vocabulary

a In the box below there are a number of useful phrases and idioms from the texts, all to do with jobs and work. Using a dictionary if necessary, make sure you understand when to use the phrases.

took a (BSc)   graduate-recruitment fairs
promoted to   draw up a check-list
regular customers   refresher course
carry out an in-depth inspection
give a talk   be at (your) desk
open-door policy   travel itinerary
take the minutes   keeps (me) up to date

b Complete the sentences below, using one phrase from the box above in each space.

1 My day officially starts at 9 p.m., but I like to be *at my desk* by 8.30.

2 If senior managers want to improve communications with their colleagues, it is a good idea for them to have an ....

3 My trip to Slovakia, Poland and Russia was quite complicated, so I asked Kim to prepare a .... for me.

4 Before you go on holiday, it's a good idea to .... of things to remember, like passports and travellers' cheques.

5 Companies often hold .... in universities and colleges, in order to attract young people into the company.

6 If you .... at a meeting, it is not necessary to write down everything that is said.

7 When I go to a foreign country, I always like to read the local newspapers, as it .... with what's happening there.

8   After leaving school at eighteen, she .... at Southampton University.

9   It is a good idea for even the most experienced staff to go on a .... occasionally, so that they do not get stale and bored.

10 If you have to .... to a group of people, you should try to find out as much as you can about them beforehand.

11 Our research shows that last year 65% of the people who stayed in the hotel were .... , whereas 35% were staying there for the first or second time.

12 It is ironic that most of the best teachers get .... administrative jobs, for which they have never been trained.

13 I was asked to visit the restaurant, ... , and then send a report on what I found to the local council.

C Work in pairs.

STUDENT A: take the part of one of the women in the articles in 14.2. Answer Student B's questions according to the information in the article. You can invent details if you want.

STUDENT B: using the collocations and phrases in 14.2, ask Student A questions about their job.

Example:

What time do you like to be at your desk?

Then reverse your roles, so that Student B takes the role of the other woman in 14.2, and Student A asks the questions.

14.4 Grammar – noun combinations

a In the texts in 14.2, there are many examples of nouns joined together in various ways. In the list below, there are three basic ways of joining nouns, with two examples of each. Find the pairs that are joined in the same way, and describe how they are joined.

Laura

food factories
safety boots
part of the job

Susan

Duncan's diary
Susan's day
briefs for meetings

b Look at the quiz about noun combinations. How many can you answer? If you need help, the answers are on page 160 – but mixed up!

1   Why do you say *a man's leg* but *a table leg*?

2   Why do you say *chicken soup* but *a chicken's egg*?

3   Why do you say *the Sunday paper* but *last Sunday's paper*?

4   Why can you say both *the side of the road* and *the roadside* (or *road-side*), but you cannot say both *the side of the desk* and *the deskside*?

5   Why do you say *a cup of coffee* but *a coffee cup*?

6   Why do you say *the treetop* but *at the top of the stairs*?

7   What's the difference between *the dog food* and *the dog's food*?

8   Is there any difference between *Turkey's history* and *the history of Turkey*?

9   True or false: if you use the *'s* construction (e.g. *John's job*), you always mean that the first noun has or owns the second noun.

10 Why can you say both *the Minister's departure* and *the departure of the Minister* but you cannot say both *the Minister's tie* and *the tie of the Minister*?

11 True or false: *a girl from Edinburgh* is the same as *an Edinburgh girl*.

C Look at the following story. Find ten mistakes in the way the nouns are combined, and correct them.

This is a true story told by Simon Bates, a personality of the TV who was well-known in Britain. His first job working in the media had been as a disc jockey on a music's station in Australia. This must have been in the early 1960s. Although Bates was a Sydney man, he started working for a small station way out in the outback, where the audience consisted of about 20 sheep's farmers and about ten million sheep. Most of the time, especially in the night middle, he was the only person present at the station, and did everything – played the records, read out the adverts for farm equipment and beer, introduced the programmes, washed the cups of tea, everything. And he was completely alone for hours at a time. *(5, 10, 15)*

Anyway, one evening, the programme of Bates was going along as usual, and he had just put a record on the player of records (no tapes or compact discs in those days!) when he suddenly desperately needed to go to the bathroom. It was actually quite a long record (*Hotel California* by the Eagles), so he decided he had enough time to get to the bathroom and back before the record's end. So off he went, leaving *Hotel California* playing to the wastes of the Australian outback. *(20, 25)*

But when he came back from the bathroom, he realised that, just after he had gone off, the record player's needle had stuck. So the audience had been hearing the same phrase from the song over and over again for five minutes. Bates sighed, sat back and waited for the angry phone's calls... *(30)*

(14.5) Collocations

a Combine one word from column A with one word in column B to make thirteen collocations to do with work. Then match each one with a definition from column C. The first one has been done as an example.

A	B	C
shop	site	a system whereby some workers work during the day and others during the night
trade	scheme	the men and women employed in a factory
customer	floor	activities within a company by which some people try to get an advantage over others
management	shop	a very large show of goods
staff	address	the wages a person earns
shift	politics	a collection of information about your clients which is held on computer
sweat	fair	the area in a factory where the ordinary workers do their work
work	packet	a system in which a company and its workers contribute money to provide a pension for ex-employees
pay	shortages	the place on a computer where you send electronic communications
e-mail	database	a factory where people are employed in bad conditions for low pay
web	force	a person learning to run a company
office	trainee	a lack of (good) personnel in a company
pension	work	the place on the internet where a company or person can be contacted for information

b Are there any more collocations to do with work that you could make using the words from columns A and B?

(14.6) Pronunciation – compound words

a A compound word is one which can be divided into two words, each of which exists in English. Look at the following list of compound words and divide them into two groups according to where the main stress comes.

workforce   pay packet   loudspeaker

sweatshop   daily paper   current affairs

trade fair   commercial break

absent-minded   tea cup   cold-blooded

pension scheme   first-class

 b Now listen to the compound words in complete sentences and check your answers.

1 Let's hope the deal is acceptable to the workforce!

2 I don't think your pay packet will be much affected.

3 We need a big loudspeaker in the corner.

4 It's no good turning the place into a sweatshop.

5 I don't usually read a daily paper unless I'm on a train or something. I'm not that interested in current affairs.

6 The trade fair is the quickest way to meet the largest number of potential customers.

7 When there's a really popular programme on TV, everybody makes a cup of tea during the commercial break, so there's an enormous demand for electricity!

8 My husband's so absent-minded he often uses a tea cup to measure out his cornflakes.

9 A police spokeswoman said it was a case of cold-blooded murder.

10 Employers increasingly see a pension scheme as an attractive extra to offer their staff.

11 The conference itself wasn't very interesting, but the accommodation was first-class.

(14.7) Listening

a Look at the diagrams below. In pairs, discuss what they might refer to.

b Listen to the conversation and make corrections on the charts.

(14.8) Writing – ordering an argument

One of the most common forms of writing is one in which you put forward arguments for and against a point of view.

You have been asked to write a 'for and against' piece on one of the following statements:

'We should try to reduce the working week as much as possible.'

OR 'There should be a legal minimum wage.'

OR 'People need to work.'

Do you agree? Put forward arguments for and against.

a A good way to start is either by discussion or, if you are working alone, by brainstorming. (See 2.9 for an example of how to brainstorm.) Make a list of at least three arguments in favour of the statement and three against it.

b Decide how you are going to organise the arguments into a logical and comprehensible structure. Using each point to form a paragraph, write the piece in rough form.

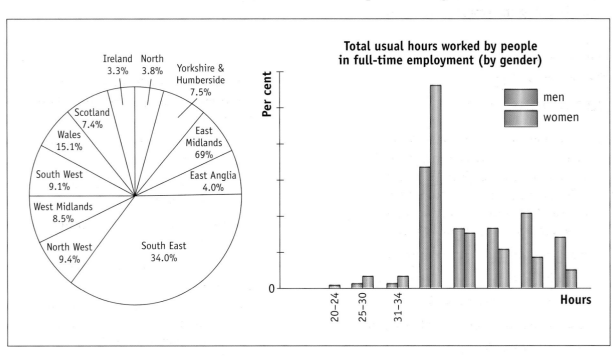

c Exchange your completed text with another group or student. Comment on their text by answering the following questions. Do not correct the English in their text unless there is something you do not understand.

1 Could the organisation of the text be improved? How?

2 Are there any points which are not clear?

3 Does the text give examples, and if so, are they relevant?

d Give the text back to the other group. Read their comments on your text. Do you agree with them?

e Reread your own text. In the light of your rereading, and the other group's comments, rewrite the text. At the same time, make any corrections to the English of your own text.

f Reread your text again. Make any final corrections and improvements. Then decide – in consultation with your teacher – what you are going to do with your finished text.

(14.9) ## Review

Complete the following passage with words from Unit 13.

Ken Brown – Inventor Extraordinaire

Ever since he was a child, Ken had been interested in mechanical things. I suppose he must have ..*taken after*.. (1) his grandfather, who was a sort of inventor though he never g .... r .... t .... (2) patenting any of the weird and wonderful things he spent his days working on in his shed at the bottom of the garden!

I think the crucial point was when Ken w .... d .... w .... (3) a very bad dose of flu and spent about a month off school. It was just after that that he c .... u .... w .... (4) his first invention – the 'Bed Bookstead'. He had been lying in bed trying to read but his arms kept getting tired. That's when it d .... o .... (5) him that many bedridden people must be in a similar predicament.

His second invention, the 'Anti-Snoring Device', d .... b .... (6) to 1995 when he and a group of friends had a

b .... - d .... (7) in a minibus in the Scottish Highlands and had to spend the night huddled together to keep warm. Apparently, one of the friends snored so much Ken didn't get a wink of sleep all night! Ken promised to invent a cure and, as we all know, it's now a best-seller (perhaps because of the entertaining a .... c .... (8) that was used to promote it).

Ken is a remarkable man. He has now been b .... o .... (9) inventions at the rate of at least ten a year for the last decade! So, how does he do it? 'Well, I usually just go down to the shed, sit down in Grandad's old armchair and wait for a flash of inspiration,' says our modest hero.

And now, of course, Ken Brown is a h .... n .... (10) whose inventions are sold all over the world. I'm sure his grandfather would be proud of the lad!

It makes you laugh

15.1 To start you thinking

a In pairs or groups, look at the cartoons below. Which make you laugh? Why? Which don't you like? Why not?

"*Arthur loves his new job with the fairground – gets a company car as well*"

"If you got a mobile phone, they wouldn't know where to send the bill."

"Not at these prices, this is a wedding anniversary, not some celebration!"

"Whatever you do, don't tell Mom he's here."

b Talk to a different group of people. Find out if they know and like the same comedians or comedy shows you like, such as Laurel and Hardy, Tom and Jerry, Mr Bean, someone from your country.

141

Reading

a Here is the headline from an article you are going to read:

BLAME A BAD JOKE ON THE BRAINWAVES

Write down five nouns and five verbs which you predict will appear in the article. When you have finished, compare your predictions with a partner. Be ready to explain your predictions.

b Read the following statements, then skim through the article below and decide if the statements are true or false.

1 Dr Katz is only one of many academics who have done research into humour.

2 He has built a machine which can tell jokes.

3 He thinks professional comedians don't really understand why humour works.

Blame a bad joke on the brainwaves

A horse walks into a bar, sits down and orders a drink. The bartender says to the horse: 'Hey Buddy, why the long face?'

Is that funny? And if it is, why? Using new techniques for studying how the brain works, Dr Bruce Katz at the University of Sussex thinks he has the answer – and hopes that he may be able to save comedians an awful lot of misery.

According to Dr Katz, humour is no laughing matter: 'If I tell you a joke, I can change your blood pressure, your heart rate, your skin response – and also give you a lot of pleasure. With just a certain sequence of sentences I can radically alter your mental and physical state.'

Despite this astonishing effect, academics have tended to turn up their noses at research into humour. What little has been done suggests that jokes are based on so-called incongruity resolution. According to this, the listener is told of a situation that naturally suggests one outcome, but another one is given instead. Only if the second outcome is still consistent with the original situation is the whole statement 'funny'.

This explains why the bartender asking 'Why the pointed ears?' is not funny even though it is just as incongruous as 'long face'. It has no connection with the concept of going into a bar looking for consolation.

But the theory does not explain why incongruity by itself can make us laugh, why timing is so important – or why humour is pleasurable.

Dr Katz believes the answer to all these lies in the way brain cells – neurons – respond to stimuli. Using a computer, he has built a very simple model of a collection of neurons and studied how they respond to jokes. Dr Katz used his model to analyse an exchange between two of the Marx Brothers that, according to Groucho, produced one of their biggest laughs:

Chico: The garbage man is here.
Groucho: Tell him we don't want any.

According to Dr Katz's model, Chico's statement triggers activity in the neurons that link his words to the concept of garbage being removed. But before that activity dies away, Groucho has jumped in, this time activating neurons that tie his statement to the incongruous idea of garbage being delivered.

For a moment, both sets of brain cells are active, producing a peak in activity – and, says Dr Katz, the pleasure of the joke.

He points out that unlike previous explanations of humour, this one shows timing is crucial: 'The second part of the statement must be in place before the brain activity triggered by the first has died away.' But it also explains why incongruity alone – such as the famous shark stuck through the roof of a house in East Oxford – can also be funny.

According to Dr Katz, the initial brain activity is created by the expectation of seeing merely terraced houses.

Seeing the incongruous shark triggers a boost in brain activity. For a moment the brain is being stimulated by both the expectation of ordinary houses and the sight of the shark, resulting in an activity peak.

Dr Katz's research opens up the possibility of one day using computers to analyse comedy scripts to see which jokes work and which don't.

'Comedians' own theories about it are usually pretty naive,' says Dr Katz. 'They also say they have no idea why some nights they die while on others the audience thinks they're the world's funniest person. One day my research could be used by those planning to invest millions in comedy movies.'

c Now read the article again more carefully and decide if the following statements are true or false.

1 The writer of the article wonders if it's funny for a horse to walk into a bar, sit down and ask for a drink.

2 If a joke is funny, your blood pressure goes up.

3 Humour is an area few academics have been keen to study.

4 Dr Katz is the first person to have explained jokes as being the result of 'incongruity resolution'.

5 If the bartender had asked 'Why the pointed ears?', it would have been just as incongruous, and therefore just as funny, as 'Why the long face?'

6 Dr Katz believes humour is achieved when two sets of a person's brain cells are activated almost simultaneously.

7 The Marx Brothers' joke shows that timing is a key element in creating humour.

8 The famous shark in the roof of a terraced house in Oxford is a good example of 'incongruity resolution'.

9 This research indicates that one day computers could be used to generate jokes which are sure to work.

10 Dr Katz thinks his research might be very useful to comedy film producers in the future.

15.3 Vocabulary

Find words or phrases in the article in 15.2 which have the same, or almost the same, meaning as the words below. The words are in the same order as in the article.

1 friend
2 sad look
3 extreme unhappiness
4 change
5 very surprising
6 avoid (because distasteful)
7 result
8 rubbish
9 cause to happen
10 gradually disappear
11 intervene quickly
12 highest point
13 extremely important
14 create
15 fail to be funny

15.4 Collocations

a Match each word in column A with its partner in column B to form common collocations connected with humour. The first one has been done as an example.

A	B
1 black	a comedian
2 practical	b entendre
3 belly	c routine
4 wry	d joke
5 punch	e crack
6 laughing	f humour
7 double	g laugh
8 wise-	h act
9 slap-	i smile
10 stand-up	j stock
11 double	k stick
12 comedy	l line

b Using some of the collocations in part a, complete the following sentences.

1 Kevin's terrible at telling jokes, he always forgets the ....!

2 Bill's stupid remarks make him a .... at work.

3 My friends put a wet towel in the bed as a ....

4 Ruth is rather reserved; even the funniest jokes only get a .... out of her.

5 Many jokes are based on a ...., where a word or phrase can be understood in two different ways.

6 .... is really a way of laughing at the more unpleasant facts of life, like death or disease.

7 Harry's such a jolly chap. His booming .... gets everybody else laughing.

8 Laurel and Hardy are probably the most famous comedy ....in the world.

9 Their type of visual, physical humour is known as ....

10 Sue's got a great sense of humour. She's always coming out with clever little ....

15.5 Learner training

a The scale below is another visual way of recording vocabulary. Put the verbs in the box in the best places on the scale (see the examples).

> chuckle ~~guffaw~~ ~~giggle~~ chortle
> titter laugh hoot cackle snigger

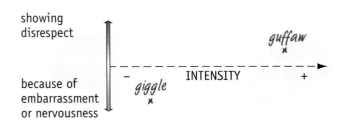

Then complete the sentences with a suitable verb – more than one verb is sometimes possible.

1 Lou sat on the sofa reading the article, ... quietly to himself every now and then.

2 I was rather offended when the children .... at my new haircut.

3 Barry .... with delight when I told him the good news.

4 The old person sat in the kitchen .... at all the latest scandalous gossip.

5 Some of the pupils sat at the back .... nervously during the lessons on sex education.

b In pairs, invent five situations (or recall some real situations) in which people laugh in a certain way.

Example:
Your teacher comes to class wearing socks of different colours. → snigger

When you have finished, join up with another pair and take it in turns to read out your situations. The other pair suggests the appropriate laugh words and **laughs in that way!**

15.6 Reading

a The following extracts come from a book about humour. First read the three statements, then skim through the information and check whether the statements are true or false.

1 The author sees humour as an amiable decoration on life – an extra bit of fun but not something central to it.

2 To appreciate humour fully, a person needs some degree of knowledge of the world.

3 When listening to a joke, we are often expected to suspend our real moral principles. This is why jokes should be 'announced' before they start.

Explaining the joke

Though nothing suffocates humour more swiftly than a thesis, the comic muse will never lack
5 commentators. Sooner or later, acknowledging the futility of the enterprise, we are all drawn to this challenge: **explain the joke**. The need to explain
10 becomes an obsession rooted in our common lot. Together with the mathematical gift, the gripping thumb, the ability to make tools, humour is a
15 specifying characteristic of humanity. For many of us, it is more than an amiable decoration on life; it is a complex piece of equipment for
20 living, a mode of attack and a line of defence, a method of raising questions and criticising arguments, a protest against the inequalities of life, a way of
25 atonement and reconciliation, a treaty with all that is wilful, impaired, beyond our power to control.

In short, humour is a serious
30 business, a land for which the explorer must equip himself thoughtfully. He must try to explain what it is that makes one pursuit of all joking, from high
35 comedy to the low snigger, and one family of all jokers, from the deft verbal designers of fiction and poetry down to the aerosol masters of back walls and
40 bridge arches.

STAGES OF EXPLANATION

Material facts
Humour nearly always supposes some piece of factual knowledge
45 shared by humorists and audience. It may be a matter of common historical information, e.g. that Henry VIII had six wives, or that Lincoln was assassinated in a
50 theatre. (*But apart from that, Mrs Lincoln, how did you enjoy the show?*) More often, however, it is simply a question of domestic acquaintance with the world.
55

Logic and likelihood
Jokers are in the habit of putting up circus-hoops through which their clients must obligingly leap, to achieve the reward of laughter.
60 The hoops are called 'does this follow?' and 'is this likely?', and as we pass through them we obediently discard our notions of logic and likelihood. Yet the assent
65 we give to the absurdities of a joke is no more contemptible than the licence we allow to the inventions of a fairy story. In the transaction of any tall tale, there is an
70 **executant**, who fixes the rules, and a **respondent**, who accepts the conditions offered, and paradoxically allows himself to be tricked in order to enjoy the
75 superiority of the insight. A joke can be a perverse experience, psychologically the understanding is degraded so that it may rise again.
80

The directive of form
Jokes are often announced, sometimes with a crude forewarning signal ('Have you heard this one?'; 'Do you know the
85 one about…?'), sometimes more subtly. However, if the intention to joke is not clearly signalled, making a sort of contract between the executant and respondent,
90 laughter is compromised. We have all had the experience of sensing humour in something heard or read, yet not being quite sure whether laughter would be a
95 respectable act or a confession of our own moral deformities. The doubt usually exists because the humorous intention has not been formally announced.
100

Language
Next we come to laughter, the trigger that detonates the humorous mass. About its functions, two things may be noted
105 at this point. One is that there is usually a centre of energy, some word or phrase in which the whole matter of the joke is fused, and from which its powers radiate; and
110 the other is that the language of humour dances most often on the points of some dual principle, an ambiguity, an overt appearance and a covert reality. Thus, the
115 hoary old riddle, *What's a Greek urn? – About 500 drachmas a week*, has its humorous centre in the word *urn*, punning with *earn*.

b Now answer the following questions. When you have finished, discuss your answers in small groups.

1 Why is humour associated with the mathematical gift and the ability to make tools?

2 What do you think has compelled the author to write this thesis even though he admits 'nothing suffocates humour more swiftly'?

3 In what way could humour be seen as a defence mechanism?

4 What do you think the 'aerosol masters of back walls and bridge arches' do? (line 38)

5 In the joke 'But apart from that, Mrs Lincoln, how did you enjoy the show?' what does *that* refer to? (line 51)

6 Why does the listener allow himself to be made a fool of by the joke-teller?

7 What similarity does the author see between listening to a fairy tale and listening to a joke?

8 What two roles does the author identify in the telling of 'tall tales'?

9 What feelings might a listener have if the humorist does not 'announce' a joke before telling it?

10 The author identifies two important points about the language used in jokes. What are they?

15.7 Grammar – fronting for dramatic effect

a Look at this sentence from the article in 15.2:

Only if the second outcome is still consistent with the original situation is the whole statement 'funny'.

Rewrite the sentence beginning with *The whole statement...*

Compare the word order. Do you notice any unusual differences?

Inversion
In the original sentence, the second clause (...*is the whole statement 'funny'*) has an unusual word order. The verb (*is*) comes before the subject (*the whole statement*) as in a question. The position of subject and verb have been exchanged, 'inverted', because of the special type of phrase *Only if* which begins the sentence.

He'S **only** funny **when he's trying to be serious.**

Only when he's trying to be serious IS he funny.

Certain strongly negative or restrictive adverbial phrases can be moved to the front of a sentence, 'fronting', for dramatic effect, usually emphasis. The original sentence is much more dramatic than the rewritten version.

When such phrases are used to begin a sentence in this way, you have to invert the relevant subject and verb. In this example the verb is *be* and so it just swaps places with the subject. But with other verbs, you need to invert the subject and the auxiliary verb exactly like in a question.

A joke **only** WORKS **if the timing is right.**

Only if the timing is right DOES a joke WORK.

b In the following sentences, front the adverbs or adverbials which are **in bold** and make the necessary inversions and other changes.

1 We understood the joke **only after** it had been explained to us.

    Only after the joke had been ....
    explained to us did we understand it.

2 Performers must **not** tell racist or sexist jokes **under any circumstances**.

3 He had **no sooner** told one joke than he started telling another.

4 We did **not** realise it was such a tedious performance **until we had already paid**.

5 I **only** realised what she meant **several hours later**.

6 I shall **never** attempt to tell a joke when speaking in public **again**.

7 The performers were **not** in any danger **at any time during the show**.

8 People laugh at jokes like that **only in England**.

9 We had **hardly** sat down at our table when the comedian singled out Chris to be the butt of his jokes!

10 One can find the films of the hilariously funny Ugo Fantozzi **only in Italy**.

c Look at the sentences below and match them with the descriptions of meaning.

1 Lucy enjoyed the clowns.

2 It was the clowns that Lucy enjoyed.

3 It was Lucy who enjoyed the clowns.

a Implies that Lucy enjoyed the clowns more than the other people watching with her.

b Has no implied meaning.

c Implies that Lucy enjoyed the clowns more than she enjoyed the other performers.

What can you say about the differences in style?

Cleft sentences
In this type of sentence, the first clause begins with *It is…* or *It was…* followed by the subject or object, depending on which you want to emphasise. The second clause begins with a pronoun like *who*, *which*, *that*, etc. and keeps the same tense as a normal sentence.

Like the fronting above, cleft sentences allow you to reorganise a sentence to highlight important details. Cleft sentences are typical of spoken English and are more dramatic than usual constructions.

d Rewrite the sentences below as cleft sentences. Use the information in brackets to decide which part should be emphasised.

1 Peter laughed more than anyone. (Brian didn't laugh so much.)

   It was Peter who laughed more than anyone.

2 Most bad comedians lack a sense of timing. (They have a sense of humour.)

   It's a sense of timing that most bad comedians lack.

3 His crazy facial expressions always crack me up. (not his jokes.)

4 My room mate had been playing practical jokes on me all along. (not who I'd suspected.)

5 I absolutely hate performing to a large audience. (I don't mind small audiences.)

6 You're really going to miss our strange sense of humour. (You won't miss other things so much.)

7 Puppet shows were always my favourite as a child. (I didn't like other things so much.)

8 Dirty jokes always get the biggest laughs. (not clean jokes.)

15.8 Writing – achieving dramatic effect

It is sometimes important to make what you write more dramatic – when writing a story or a newspaper article, for example. There are many devices good writers use to achieve dramatic effect. Here are some of them.

● intensification/exaggeration
  e.g. very interesting → absolutely fascinating/spellbinding;
  rather dull → mindnumbingly tedious

● rhetorical questions
  e.g. Many people wonder how he has stayed in power for so long. → So, how has he managed to hang on to power for so long?

● assonance and alliteration (repeating the same sounds)
  e.g. It was a difficult walk under the desert sun. → The trek through the desert was unrelenting. It was hard. It was hot. It was heartbreaking.

● repetition (particularly three times!)
  e.g. Location is very important when looking for a house to buy. → There are three important things when buying a house – location, location and location!

● cleft sentences (see 15.7)
  e.g. When telling a joke, timing is really important. → What is really important when telling a joke is timing.

● 'fronting' of restrictive and negative adverbials (see 15.7)
  e.g. A joke only works if the timing is right. → Only if the timing is right does the joke work.

a Now look at the following review of a comedy show and make it more dramatic. Pay particular attention to the underlined sections.

Bill Blood's one-man-show is really <u>very good</u>. He stands up night after night and <u>hits</u> the audience with jokes that have them <u>laughing a lot</u> and <u>asking</u> him to stop! <u>Many people wonder why he is so funny. It may be his face or the speed at which he talks or the nervous way he moves around.</u> According to his manager, Wilbur White, those things are important but <u>timing is the most important thing of all</u>.

So, remember the name – Bill Blood. He's <u>highly entertaining</u> and he's in town for the next five days, appearing at the Apollo. <u>You mustn't miss this show under any circumstances!</u>

3 Where do you think the remainder of their imports come from?

4 What is absurd about this second non-smoking story?

5 What is the double meaning of 'is there' in the story about the platform?

6 Why was Mr Shaw in court? How plausible was his defence?

b Now compare your answers in small groups. Discuss which of the excerpts (if any) you found particularly funny. Try to decide what it is that you find funny.

(15.10) Review

Complete the sentences below with words and phrases from Unit 14.

1 Gordon, could you let me have the t.......... i.......... for my business trip to Germany?

2 They've decided to keep the factory open 24 hours a day and run a n..........-s............

3 Some of our middle managers were a bit out of touch with modern methods, so we sent them on various r.......... c.......... and it's made a tremendous difference.

4 Mrs Nelson was ill that day, so no one t.......... any m.......... for that particular meeting.

5 That clothes factory should be closed down, it's nothing but a s.......... – the workers are there from dawn to dusk and earn practically nothing.

6 The inspectors have d.......... up a c..........-l..........of the areas we have to improve on.

7 Companies run annual g..........-r.......... fairs to try to attract university leavers to their firms.

8 It can be very noisy on the s..........-f.......... of the factory so you'd better wear some ear plugs.

9 Export sales were up 25% last year so we all got a p..........-r.......... bonus for Christmas.

10 I'll never forget the day I took home my first p.......... p............ Unfortunately, I spent it all within two days!

b Think of a comedy show, comedian, author, actor or cartoonist that is your own particular favourite and write a brief review of about 120 words, explaining (dramatically) why they are so funny.

(15.9) Listening

a Read the following questions, then listen to some excerpts from a humorous radio programme and answer the questions. Each question refers to a different short news story.

1 What is absurd about the non-smoking room?

2 What do you think has happened to the crew of the lost ship?

Tapescripts

Unit 1

1.3b Vocabulary

1 **TEACHER 1:** I think it's vital we try and get more computers installed in the school. We can't start the new millennium with just two PCs.

TEACHER 2: Well, I agree, but you know it's the Head who has the final word on things like that.

2 **FRANK:** Debbie, will … will you marry me?

DEBBIE: Look, Frank, you know I think the world of you, and we'll always be friends, and I respect your judgment awfully …

FRANK: In other words, you don't want to marry me.

DEBBIE: But Frank you've got to understand that I want to go on seeing you, but I see our relationship as like brother and sister …

3 (on the telephone)

OFFICE WORKER: Will all this stuff be ready by Tuesday?

COURIER FIRM MAN: Yes, of course. I give you my word.

OFFICE WORKER: You said that about the last delivery, and that was three days late.

4 **CAL:** I'm going to see Mrs Pringle about a pay rise this afternoon.

DONNA: Are you? Well, I warn you, she's in a pretty bad mood today.

CAL: Oh. Look, I know I shouldn't ask you this, but … could you put in a good word for me at the Departmental meeting this morning?

DONNA: Why should I do that?

CAL: Well, you know how hard I've been working, putting in long hours, that sort of thing.

DONNA: Look, Cal, this is none of my business, you should go and see her yourself.

5 **EDWARD:** There's a story going round that Douggie's boy has been … arrested.

IAN: Arrested? What for?

EDWARD: They say he was caught forging signatures on company cheques.

IAN: I don't believe a word of it. That boy hasn't got the courage to cross the road on his own, let alone do anything criminal.

6 **1ST SPEAKER:** Good match, then?

2ND SPEAKER: Hm, I really have to eat my words on that one.

1ST SPEAKER: How do you mean?

2ND SPEAKER: I'd said that Liverpool would win two-nil.

1ST SPEAKER: Yeah? What made you think that?

2ND SPEAKER: Well, they destroyed them when they played them last month.

1ST SPEAKER: And what was the final score?

2ND SPEAKER: One all. Liverpool went out on away goals.

7 (on the telephone)

REP: Thank you very much for calling Sun Life Widows Insurance. May I ask you how you heard about us?

CUSTOMER: Word of mouth – a friend of mine told me about you, so I thought I'd give you a ring.

REP: And we're very glad you did. Now if there's any more information you'd like …

8 **RADIO VOICE:**
Attitudes to the whole field of advertising have changed enormously over the past few years. Up until, say, 20 years ago, 'advertising' had always been a dirty word in Britain. It was associated with a rather American approach to the world of business. But that's all changed now – advertising is seen as a dynamic, fashionable area to be in – especially if you call it 'marketing'.

9 **1ST MAN:** Don't you think that Weaver's been working a bit too hard lately? He's always here until well past six o'clock, and I know he takes work home with him. I'm worried about his health.

2ND MAN: I'll have a word in his ear. No need to tell the whole world.

10 **ARTIST:** Well, there it is. Five years of work. What do you think?

WOMAN: It's … it's … I'm lost for words, Arturo, I really am.

ARTIST: What do you think about the blue patch in the corner? It's a symbol of freedom, you see. Freedom of the spirit.

WOMAN: Five years, did you say? That long?

Unit 2

2.5b Listening

2.7 Hearing perception

VOICE 1: About a year ago I had a violent reaction to something I ate. 'My first allergy,' I thought. Earlier this century any such reaction was referred to as an allergy, but not now says Dr Jonathon Brostov, physician in charge of the Allergy Clinic at the Middlesex Hospital in London.

VOICE 2: People say that if they're affected by something, they must be allergic, but, strictly speaking, food allergy has a definable immunological response, the reaction is quick – put a peanut on your lip and you swell. Skin tests are positive, blood test is positive and it's really very easy to diagnose because the patient tells you the diagnosis.

VOICE 1: Classical food allergies are clearly detectable by the presence of specific antibodies called IGE in the blood. The most common culprits are milk, eggs, shellfish, fish and peanuts. But there's also a less dramatic reaction to food, what doctors call food intolerance.

VOICE 2: Food intolerance is 'mechanism unknown', *although it may be immunological* because you do have thirty feet of intestine* and it's difficult to know what happens* all the way down there.* The reactions are much slower, *it's usually the 'total load', *you eat a lot of particular food. *And the diseases are those perhaps a little bit indeterminate, *migraine, irritable bowel, *achy joints, * 'I don't feel well', *'I'm tired' *but also diseases such as Crohn's Disease, *rheumatoid arthritis, eczema *– all affected by food, *possibly by immunological mechanisms, possibly not.*

VOICE 1: Most often people are intolerant to common foods such as wheat, yeast and dairy products – foods they consume every day, little realising they're aggravating or even causing their symptoms … Orthodox medical opinion is often sceptical about food sensitivities, especially food intolerance. Patients with vague symptoms are easily fobbed off by their GPs and labelled neurotic. They may turn to alternative forms of testing and treatment – hair strand analysis, kinesiology and others, sometimes with effective results, others less so.

Unit 3

3.11 Listening

3.12 Hearing perception

FEMALE REPORTER: No, that's not the wrong tape. I **am** in Florida. About half an hour's drive northwest of Tampa. I've come up on Route 19, which is about as unattractive an American highway as I've ever seen. But just off that main road is this small old-fashioned town of Tarpon Springs and right in the middle is a big church, which, to my surprise, is Greek Orthodox!

YOUNGER LOCAL MAN: Coming here to Tarpon Springs *is like having a place you could call *Athens with a zip code. *It is as if you are in Greece, *there are people here after forty years *who still speak Greek and know perhaps a few words of English. *There are times when you become confused, *you step outside of the church *after the rituals of incense and worship and prayer *and you expect to be on a Greek island *and down the street becomes the confusing part when you have um *the prefabrication of American shopping malls, etc.

FEMALE REPORTER: One in three of the population here is Greek. I'm standing outside the Parthenon Bakery on Athens Street and inside the locals are speaking Greek amongst themselves and they really seem to revel in all things Greek.

LOCAL WOMAN: I'd say that now our customs are probably more traditional than they are in Greece because the people came here, they had their traditions when they left in the early nineteen hundreds and they never changed. The men get preferential treatment in families; if there are boys, they come first. They're spoiled. Yeah, it's kind of like a time-warp, I guess. Yeah.

OLDER LOCAL MAN: Here on the right we have the Greek traditional coffee shop, men only.

FEMALE REPORTER: Men only in nineteen ninety nine in the United States? This doesn't seem possible!

OLDER LOCAL MAN: You('ve) got to remember you're in Tarpon Springs, it's a great village and the Greek man, I think you can call him a chauvinist. This is a place for the men to gather and in Tarpon Springs it was where all the sponge divers and all the crews and everyone gathered. You play cards, there's a lot of camaraderie. It's just a place for men only. In nineteen ninety nine. Ha ha.

Unit 4

4.10 Listening

VOICE 1: And on this particular occasion, which was quite late in December, um … my colleague, Matt, and I were out in a car and we were sent to a ram-raid in progress, which obviously means it's happening at the time. Anyway, we came round the corner and, sure enough, embedded in this shop front is a car and outside the shop facing towards us is another car, quite a big estate car with its lights on. And, as we pulled up, the estate car pulled off towards us and was coming pretty much head-on. And I was driving, managed to swerve to one side and it just sort of caught the wing of our car and carried on going up on the pavement and passed us. And then out of the shop came two other people and they were wearing balaclavas and red Santa hats with bobbles, and they ran out and we stopped our car and then we both grabbed a person each and we were both wrestling with our prisoners, trying to gain control of them. Matt suddenly started screaming and I looked up to see the estate car that had pulled away was blocking my view of him and I could only hear him screaming and um … I shouted to him, what's the matter? And he said 'Just stay with him', meaning the person I was with and so I did but it was quite a dilemma as to whether or not to go and help him and leave my prisoner. And so in the end I decided to stay with my prisoner because I thought well, if Matt isn't seriously injured then at least I'll have caught a prisoner and if he is seriously injured, I'll want to get at least one of the people that is sort of responsible for it. So anyway eventually this estate drove away and I carried on concentrating on my prisoner and then Matt shouts, 'Get out of the road!' and I looked up to see the estate car reversing at speed towards me. And I was on my knees with my prisoner and if it had hit me, it would have been head-high, and it would have been pretty nasty but fortunately I managed to dive out of the road and drag my prisoner with me into a doorway, still scrapping. And I remember just looking up at the estate car which was sort of hovering beside me, thinking any second now these people in the car are going to come out and they're going to rescue their fourth man and at that moment another police car came round the corner and the estate drove off and I just waved at the police car to go after that car. Matt had had to let go of his prisoner and I managed to keep mine and some other officers came along and helped. Anyway, it turned out that Matt had been lying on the pavement, wrestling, and his legs were in the road and the car had come along and driven over his ankles backwards and forwards in an attempt to free their friend and fortunately he had some big boots on and um … he managed to get away with just bruises, which was quite amazing cos there's some pretty impressive tyre marks over his boots, which he's kept for posterity. And the car that was being chased, the estate car, which by this time had three people in it, with Matt's prisoner, had something wrong with it, so they had to abandon it a few yards down the road. And two of them ran off and were quickly caught and one ran up on to the rooftops and was chased by a dog handler and his dog, amazingly, on the rooftops but then they went down a very big drop to a very low rooftop and he'd have injured the dog if he'd let the dog go down there; so the officer put a special harness on to the dog and lowered it down on to the lower roof and um … and then jumped down himself and they managed to get the fourth man. And so they were all arrested and they all went to court and they all got three years in prison.

VOICE 2: And you got an award. Is that right?

VOICE 1: Yeah, Matt and I got a commendation for bravery because we'd sort of been ruthless and held on to our prisoners despite being injured.

Unit 5

5.8 Idioms

1   MAN 1: Do you fancy going parachuting some time?
    MAN 2: Parachuting? *Parachuting?*
    You must be joking! I wouldn't go parachuting for all the tea in China …
    MAN 1: Afraid, are we?
    MAN 2: You bet I am! What happens if the thing doesn't open?

2   WOMAN: Good journey home, dear?
    MAN: Since you ask, no. The train was 45 minutes late, and then we were packed like sardines into the carriage.
    WOMAN: Lucky you had a shower this morning, then.
    MAN: Unfortunately, that wasn't true of the people crushed up against me …

3   WOMAN: Of course, he's a lovely man, but as nutty as a fruitcake.
    MAN: Really? You mean he's a bit on the odd side?
    WOMAN: Well, more than odd, I'd say. He keeps his slippers in the fridge. Says he likes to keep his feet cool.
    MAN: That's not so much eccentric as completely loony.
    WOMAN: Well, there you go.

4   WOMAN: How was last night?
    MAN: All right. John made a pig of himself, as usual.

WOMAN: Did he? Perhaps he hadn't had anything to eat at lunchtime.

MAN: Oh yes he had! He went out with Marie-Claude at lunchtime to that new brasserie in Lamb Street.

5 WOMAN: Did you know that Frank's become a really big cheese in the EU?

MAN: Frank? What, Frank Parsons? That little squit in the Research Department?

WOMAN: Yes, he's become something like Deputy Head of the Department of Statistics, or Information.

MAN: Does he have to live in Brussels, then?

WOMAN: Mmm, well, he has a flat there, and comes back home at weekends.

6 MAN 1: Have you seen this new programme on Channel 4? The one with the two men who live on a boat.

MAN 2: 'Men Boating Badly', you mean? Oh God yes, and I've bought all the videos as well.

MAN 1: Oh, you haven't! It's not that good!

MAN 2: It is! As far as I'm concerned, it's the best thing since sliced bread.

7 WOMAN 1: Liz has got a new job on the Newcastle Evening Post.

WOMAN 2: What, you mean she's moving from London?

WOMAN 1: Yup! from March.

WOMAN 2: A bad move, I'd say. No journalist worth their salt would work outside London.

WOMAN 1: I disagree! There's plenty going on in Newcastle.

WOMAN 2: That's not the point. London is where the *important* things happen …

8 MAN 1: And you can see all around you that the standard of living is getting better all the time.

MAN 2: Absolute poppycock. The number of people living on the breadline has increased significantly since the present government came to power.

MAN 1: I'm sorry, but there is no evidence whatsoever for that assertion …

9 MAN 1: What happened, then, on Tuesday? Did you get in all right?

MAN 2: Oh God, don't talk about it. I was nearly an hour late. But luckily the boss had a meeting that morning, so she never saw me come in. And then later Carol really saved my bacon by telling her I came in on time that day.

MAN 1: Blimey! That was good of her. Why'd she do that, then?

MAN 2: Dunno. Must fancy me.

10 WOMAN 1: Don't you think this means the end of the whole operation? Now that Brookes has gone, we'll have to change everything.

WOMAN 2: No, I don't think that, actually. But his decision to resign has certainly given us food for thought.

WOMAN 1: Food for thought! Is that all you can say? We've got to *do* something!

5.9 Hearing perception

And it's one of those restaurants *that you see all over France *where basically they offer a menu for that day *which means you have no choice about what you eat *you just turn up and buy the menu *this was a fifty franc menu *and the first thing that happened when you walk into the restaurant and sit down is that they just *well … paper cloth on the table and they put *a large bottle of red wine and a large basket of bread *on the table in front of you. *Now that is a delightful way to start any meal. *For me it was almost enough! *It was then followed by a fantastic home made vegetable soup *gallons of it and every time we finished the bowl *it was refilled, because they obviously thought we wanted more *although we were desperately trying to finish it not to be rude and leave some *we didn't realise the etiquette of the situation.

Unit 6

6.8 Listening

MALE RADIO HOST: And now just rounding up the financial news this Tuesday evening …

The Footsie One Hundred Share Index has just closed up 10 points at 3860. That's a rise of about 40 points since this time last week so things are definitely looking better.

The Dow Jones is also rallying, though trading is still in progress. At yesterday's close, it stood at 5564 and looks to be on the way up again today.

Surprisingly, the Nikkei closed unchanged from Monday.

Turning now to have a look at how the pound is faring against other currencies. It's slightly up (by half a cent) against the dollar; steady at 161 Yen; and still gaining ground against the German mark – you'll need 2.31 Deutschmarks to buy a pound today.

A few tourist rates for people on the move. A pound will buy you 7.5 French francs, 186.4 Spanish pesetas, 2,365 Italian lire and 2.2 Aussie dollars.

And finally, some late-breaking news. The giant Hassington Bank has made a friendly offer to take over Middlehampton Building Society. Needless to say, the Middlehampton share price rocketed by nearly £2 to finish the day at 368 pence – up from 178 pence!

H P Lang – the building conglomerate – turned in very small six-monthly profits of £2.4 million, causing their share price to tumble from 295 pence to 190 pence at close of trading and they may slip further tomorrow.

That's it for now. Back to you, Sally.

FEMALE RADIO HOST: Thanks a lot, Gavin. Now continuing our investigation into mortgage rates …

Unit 7

7.7 Listening

7.8 Hearing perception

INTERVIEWER: And um what **is** a bush baby exactly? Could you describe …?

PENNY: Well, it's actually related to humans, distantly. It's a prosimian, which is a primate and related to things like lemurs.

INTERVIEWER: Right.

PENNY: It's on a different branch of the primate family from monkeys. Monkeys have got dry noses and they've got … galagos and lemurs have got wet noses, rather like a cat or a dog. So they're distinguished by that.

INTERVIEWER: Healthy ones.

PENNY: Well yes, the healthy ones. They're small. *The largest are about squirrel-size *and the smallest are about as big as a hamster. *And they tend to have big ears and very big eyes *because, as I said, they're nocturnal and they need their big eyes in the dark. *And they're distinguished as primates *because they've got clasping hands (Right) *and instead of claws they've got nails, like we have, finger nails *and various other things like forward-looking vision and an upright posture.*

INTERVIEWER: And do they … ?

PENNY: They live in the trees. (Right) *Different levels, depending on the species. *But they live in the trees and they tend to get around *not by running along the branches but by *leaping and then clinging. *So, well, they'll jump from one tree to the next and hang on. *And they catch insects, they live on insects *and they catch them with their hands, grasping the insect.

INTERVIEWER: Right. So they live in family groups, like other primates, or … ?

PENNY: Well, that's a good question. Um, apparently, I don't know, perhaps I'll be able to observe this but I'm told that the females and the young have a small territory each and that the males tend to have larger territories that overlap with different females.

INTERVIEWER: Right. And this is your first sort of trip like this.

PENNY: Yes, it is. It's very exciting.

INTERVIEWER: So who's sort of sponsoring all this?

PENNY: It's the … there's a name for it, there's an organisation, the Primate … I've forgotten the name.

It's a primate group, the Primate Study Group, or something like that. Based at Oxford Uni … no, Brookes University and um the purpose is to go and try and find out different species by their sounds or to find out whether their sounds indicate that they're a different species or not. So we not only have to record them, but we also have to trap them and weigh them and measure them and take photographs of them and try and identify them and then … I believe we take hair because you can get DNA readings off their hair but we're not going to harm them, we're going to let them go again.

INTERVIEWER: Right.

PENNY: This is why I've had to have rabies jabs because I'll be handling animals and they might bite.

INTERVIEWER: Hmm. You've already had those?

PENNY: I've had one.

INTERVIEWER: Ah, it's a series.

PENNY: Mmm.

INTERVIEWER: Nasty?

PENNY: Not too bad, not too bad.

INTERVIEWER: OK. Well, thank you very much.

Unit 8

8.9a Pronunciation – word-class pairs

ADVERTISEMENT 1: Do you miss the good old days when fruit and veg were really fresh? Well, at Bolton's of Ipswich, we can promise you the freshest produce in town. And look at these prices. Braeburn apples 80 pence a pound, fresh British strawberries one pound a punnet, Spanish broccoli 52 pence a pound. Bolton's of Ipswich – at 18 Queen Street, Ipswich. All prices subject to change without notice.

ADVERTISEMENT 2: Do you object to paying inflated prices for designer goods? Well, come to Bicester Shopping Village, where you can find top names in fashion, interior design and furniture at more than 20% off the High Street price! Bicester Shopping Village – it's a whole new shopping experience.

ADVERTISEMENT 3: When Chandler came back to his apartment, he noticed that something was out of place. The floor was unnaturally clean and shiny. He thought he knew who to suspect. He opened the door to his office … slowly. A sweet perfume hit him. Sitting on his desk was the culprit. Bitter. Lemony. Tangy. His floors would never be dirty again.

New Spliff floorshine. Perfect for floors. Perfect for you. From all good stores and supermarkets.

ADVERTISEMENT 4: Ah always thought of myself as an outsahder, y'know … thrown aht ah school, spent long years on the road, bit of a hobo, yah know? Bin travelling from town to town. One thing ah never changed, that's mah Southern Jeans, cos they TOUGH, man, y'know? They tell you sumping baht a man.

Southern Jeans. For the rebel in you.

ADVERTISEMENT 5: Theft and burglary from private houses is on the increase. Last year, one out of every six people suffered a break-in of some kind at home. Crime is at a record high. Make sure YOUR house is safe from burglars by installing the new Philatronic 2000 alarm system. Available from Nine oh Nine Security, Bath Street, Edinburgh.

ADVERTISEMENT 6: He was an ex-convict looking for a reason to live. **She** was an artist with a contract on her head. His job: to escort her from Washington DC to a courthouse in Texas. Her job: to stay alive for six more days.

A Justin Rivera film. *Desert Runner*. Certificate 15. In all good cinemas now.

Unit 9

9.9 Listening

Person A – Thomas

INTERVIEWER: So, what do you remember about your school days?

THOMAS: What do you mean? Good things or bad things?

INTERVIEWER: Either. Just anything that stands out in your mind.

THOMAS: Um … well. I'll never forget my first day at secondary school. It was quite a trauma for me as I'd been at a little village school up until then, in a class of ten kids, all nice and cosy really. And then all of a sudden there I was at 'big school', surrounded by hundreds of, what seemed to me at the tender age of eleven, very big boys! In the classroom there were about thirty of us. The teacher was very strict and I soon found out I was no longer called Tommy but Turner TJ – form 1B! I was in a state of shock, I suppose. I didn't really talk all day, except to say 'Yes, sir!'

Person B – Claire

INTERVIEWER: Can you tell me something about your school days, Claire?

CLAIRE: Yeah sure! They were great! Really the 'best days

of my life'. As you know, I went to Summerhill, which is, like, tooootally different from any other school. The main idea is that you go to school to prepare for life, be responsible for yourself and find inner happiness and NOT to be pushed around by small-minded teachers who just want you to pass lots of exams so their school looks good. I mean, places like that can leave a person damaged for life! No, Summerhill was brilliant. You don't have to go to lessons but you can if you want – with brilliant teachers too. You spend your time doing what *you* think is important. You don't have to take any exams. Mind you, I did and so did most of my friends. I made some really close friends, boys and girls and teachers! I'm still in touch with most of them now.

Person C – Chris

INTERVIEWER: How do you rate your school education, Chris? Did it prepare you for life?

CHRIS: That's a good question. Um … I think the short answer is a definite 'No!' Looking back, it seems incredible that there were never any discussions about careers after school. I suppose that's because the teachers had such a narrow view of life – working to the curriculum and getting pupils to pass exams. None of what I was taught seemed to have any relevance to real life. I once asked a teacher what geometry was for. He said it taught one how to solve problems. If, instead, he'd told me the word came from the Greek 'ge', the earth, and 'metron', a measure, and that the meaningless triangles I was asked to juggle with formed the basis of geographical exploration, astronomy and navigation, the subject would have immediately become much more romantic, exciting and, well, you know, appealing. So, when I left school I didn't have the faintest idea about what I wanted to do. I eventually drifted into writing and journalism based initially on my diaries of my travels around Europe after I left school with nowhere to go!

Unit 10

10.5 Listening

10.7 Hearing perception

MAN: well, anyway, I was out with the kids * y'know, took 'em for a walk *y'know, like, in the buggy * and they was howling for something to eat *so we moseys into the corner shop *y'know in Wood Green *and they're starving, y'know *so we get these Supahoops off the shelves *y'know, 33p each *daylight robbery *and well we get out of the shop *and the little nippers just rip open the bag *and then the girl starts screaming *'Daddy, Daddy! there's yucky yuck,'* but of course they're back in the buggy by now, and it's too late, I can't be bothered to go back in and make a fuss, so we're in the park, and I look in the packet, and there's this… I dunno how to describe it really, piece of crispy stuff, like fried stuff, with two black bits in it, like someone's dropped a used sticky plaster in the mix… God, I came over all funny when I saw it, cos it looked sorta DEFORMED, know what I mean? like someone's finger in there … y'know what I mean?

Anyway, course the kid's really hacked off, 'cos she's down two Supahoops, y'know, and her little bruvver's got a packet too, but 'e ain't got any yucky bits in 'is, has he? So 'e's laughing 'is 'ead orf! … and the thing is, y'know, we've been going down the shops, getting a packet of Supahoops every Sunday for YEARS, y'know, week in week out, and they've always been perfect … never been anything wrong before …

… so I promise her, like, I'll send a letter to Supahoops Limited, or whatever, and get 'er another packet, or better still, get some dosh from them, 'nuff to pay for a couple o' beers down the Pig 'n' Whistle, eh??? buy her a little dolly to make it up to her, y'know what I mean? … fair enough …

Unit 11

11.7 Listening

ANNOUNCER: Our guest on the programme today is Neil Le Power, whose book *Town and Around* has just been published. It's a survey of twelve towns and cities in England and Wales, a survey which took place over fifteen months. And Neil is here to discuss the conclusions that the researchers came to. Neil, welcome to the programme.

NEIL LE POWER: Thank you.

ANNOUNCER: Now, we've had endless reports and surveys into British towns over the last few years. What's different about yours?

NEIL LE POWER: Well, I think the main difference is that our report was based on talking to local people. As you say, we've heard many opinions expressed over the last 20 years about the decline of the British town, but these have nearly always been **experts** talking. We talked to ordinary people, over 1,000 in the twelve towns, and we also spoke to more than 300 voluntary organisations. We talked to police officers, local business people, nightclub owners, church leaders, and hundreds of individuals we just encountered in the street, or in the pub, or by arrangement in their homes.

ANNOUNCER: There's a feeling, isn't there, that things have somehow **gone wrong** with British towns. Is that what people told you?

NEIL LE POWER: Yes, broadly speaking, yes. I think we managed to identify three areas where our

correspondents felt things had gone wrong or were going wrong. The first of these was the fact that British towns are now dominated by the private car …

ANNOUNCER: Mmm, yes, I thought that was the most interesting part of the book. Because it was a missed opportunity, wasn't it?

NEIL LE POWER: Very much so. A report came out all the way back in 1963 called *Traffic in Towns* which anticipated a lot of the dangers which were threatened by the growth of car ownership, and actually put down several very sensible recommendations, but only some of these were ever acted on. For example, the very simple one that working hours should be staggered to avoid the early morning and early evening traffic jams …

ANNOUNCER: And of course, the infamous ring roads …

NEIL LE POWER: Yes, ring roads have created major psychological barriers to walking or cycling in and out of town centres even from residential areas only ten minutes' walking distance from the centre. In Preston we talked to people living on housing estates only a few minutes' walk away from the town centre who would never dream of walking … there are just too many barriers … pedestrian underpasses, tunnels, steps, broken pavements …

ANNOUNCER: Traffic lights where you have to run like a rabbit to get across in time …

NEIL LE POWER: Well, yes, there's a ring road in Northampton, where it's physically impossible to get across it in less than seven seconds, and yet the traffic is so busy that on average there's only a five second gap between the cars! And if you're a mother with a pushchair, or disabled, it's even worse. No wonder nobody walks! You get the mad situation where people who are going to the gym or the swimming pool to get fit, drive there even if it's just round the corner! In Middlesbrough, a woman told us that people used cars to travel to the next street.

ANNOUNCER: In fact, if you go to the continent, to France, or Germany, you find that city centres have been turned into pedestrian precincts, and the car's been almost banned …

NEIL LE POWER: That's right. And, of course, the person who needs to go by car is often the very person who can't! Like old women and young children. And even though everybody regards shopping as one of the great pleasures…

ANNOUNCER: Surely not!

NEIL LE POWER: … in fact, if you don't have a car, it's a nightmare.

ANNOUNCER: But most people do have a car, don't they?

NEIL LE POWER: Absolutely not. In the survey, we found that three-quarters of housewives in Milton Keynes do not have access to the family car during week-days. But of course the people who make decisions all drive cars – hardly any of the planners and politicians we visited had recently walked anywhere.

Unit 12

12.7 Listening

12.8 Hearing perception

LECTURER: The second of the two great Florentine artists who make the art of the Italian sixteenth century (or 'Cinquecento') so famous was, of course, Michelangelo Buonarroti (1475–1564). Michelangelo was 23 years younger than Leonardo and outlived him by 45 years. When he was 13 he was apprenticed for three years to the busy workshop of Domenico Ghirlandajo, one of the leading masters of the late fifteenth century. However, Michelangelo did not particularly enjoy his time in this rather traditional workshop – his ideas about art were rather different. Instead of absorbing the facile manner of Ghirlandajo, he went out to study the work of the great masters of the past, Giotto, Donatello and the Greek and Roman sculptors, who knew how to represent every detail of the human body in movement. Like Leonardo, he was not content with learning the laws of anatomy secondhand and made his own research by dissecting bodies and drawing from living models until the human body held no secrets for him. But, unlike Leonardo for whom man was only one of the fascinating puzzles of nature, Michelangelo strove with incredible singleness of purpose to master this one problem as fully as possible. His power of concentration and retentive memory must have been so great that soon there was no posture or movement which he could not draw. By the age of thirty, he was acknowledged as one of the outstanding masters of the age, equal in his way to the genius of Leonardo.

Of course, arguably his greatest work – the ceiling of the Sistine Chapel, commissioned by Pope Julius II – was something Michelangelo tried to evade by saying he was a sculptor not a painter! He started work on a modest design but suddenly changed his mind, shut himself up in the chapel, let no one come near him and started work on a plan which would, as he said, 'amaze the whole world'!

It is very difficult for us to imagine *how one human being could achieve what Michelangelo achieved *in four years of lonely work *on the scaffoldings of the papal chapel. *The physical exertion of preparing the scenes in elaborate detail *and painting this huge fresco while lying on his back *a few inches from the surface of the ceiling *and looking upwards all the time is amazing. *But this is nothing *compared to the intellectual and artistic achievement. *The richness of new inventions, *the mastery of execution in every detail *and, above all, the grandeur of the visions *which Michelangelo revealed to those who came after him, *have given mankind quite a new idea *of the power of genius.*

So, let's now look at our first slide, which is probably the most famous detail from the ceiling, 'The Creation of Adam'. Most of us, of course, have seen it so often on postcards, in books, even on CD covers that it is difficult to see it with fresh eyes. But we must try to forget what we know …

Unit 13

13.8 Listening

13.9 Hearing perception

Part 1

ANNOUNCER: Professor Harold Thimbleby is Professor of Computing Research at Middlesex University. He has campaigned for many years to make the gadgets and machines we use less complicated. Here he explains his ideas. He starts by trying to answer the question: why do people want to buy such complicated things?

PROFESSOR: Another thing … coming back to your point that we seem to want to buy these things … the evidence is, they're designed to confuse us so that we appear to want them. That's a fairly subtle point. Let's say there's a tourist company … I'll explain it in terms of tourist companies … it's a bit easier to understand the general idea. You want to go to Costa Del Sol and some hotel … you want a swimming pool, you want to be near the beach, whatever, whatever your criteria are, you've got kids and you want … so on. If you look in any travel brochure about the hotels and resorts, they tell you different things about each hotel. And pretty soon you discover you don't know how to make a decision – and you make a random decision – that's deliberate, because if you chose the best hotel everybody would go to that hotel, so what the travel companies do is they tell you 'This hotel's got a swimming pool,' they tell you 'this hotel's got, you know, access to the beach, this hotel's got children's facilities, this hotel …'. Basically, the point of that is to spread the customers out amongst the different hotels because if everybody went to the best hotel, that hotel couldn't cope and all the others would do nothing. So the purpose of the brochure isn't to help you select a hotel, it's to spread the customers amongst the hotels that they have on offer. That sort of thing goes on with video recorders. The purpose isn't to give you features you want, the purpose is to get you into the shop, confuse you so that you can be sold a product on the basis that it's a pound cheaper than a competitor's, or that it's made by a brandname that rings a bell or that, you know, it was at the front of the shop. And those are all things they know how to control. So as you look at it, you know, why are they making confusing gadgets? Well, because they sell. And they sell because confusing people is an easy way of controlling them.

Part 2

PROFESSOR: I once had hope that safety critical systems would be a way of improving things, like … we can all laugh about a video recorder, you know, at worst you record the wrong programme or whatever, you know it's just irritating and we certainly laugh about it … but that sort of gadget is also available in, for instance, aeroplane cockpits. Have you seen an aeroplane cockpit? You know, they're covered in knobs, buttons and things … or a nuclear power station, you name it, in a safety critical environment they have gone overboard in gadgets that are rather similar to video recorders … and it's then no longer a jok e… it's deadly serious. Um … I've worked with some of these interfaces and in aeroplanes,

and although it doesn't help me to say this, *my cynical view is *they are designed *not to be easy to use , *they're designed so that when the plane crashes, *the manufacturers can say *'it was the pilot's fault', *'cause of course if you blame the machine *then, you know, *thousands of aircraft have to be grounded *and you know, that's that's a big economic problem, *but if you can blame the user, *I mean, I'm I'm I'm certainly being cynical when I put it like this, *but if you can blame the user, *and if the user's killed himself, *so much the easier to blame them, *then it's **not** the machine's problem …

Unit 14

14.7 Listening

1ST MAN: So, you reckon there's a few mistakes on the charts?

WOMAN: No, not a few, there are several, look, it's a complete mess – didn't anybody check these before they handed them back?

2ND MAN: I think they were checked …

1ST MAN: Well, they are usually …

WOMAN: Oh, don't give me that, it's clear to me that no-one has looked at these.

2ND MAN: What's the problem with them?

WOMAN: Well, let's start with the pie-chart, the one with the number of businesses per region, can you see that?

1ST / 2ND MAN: Yeah, yeah.

WOMAN: Well, first of all, some of the titles of the regions are wrong. If you look at the top left, it says 'Ireland', well it should be 'Northern Ireland' of course. 'Ireland' would just mean the Irish Republic, so read 'Northern Ireland'

2ND MAN: 'cause that's part of the UK …

WOMAN: Right, thank you, and I think 'North West' and 'South West' have been transposed …

2ND MAN: They've been transposed, have they?

WOMAN: Yeah. The names, I mean. Where it says on your pie-chart 'South West nine point one' …

(**2ND MAN:** South West … oh yeah, and North West there …)

WOMAN: …well that should be 'North West nine point four', and 'South West nine point one'.

2ND MAN: That's what it says, is it?

1ST MAN: No, so hang on, no, so it should be … where it says 'South-West nine point one' that should be 'North-West'…

WOMAN: That's right.

2ND MAN: Oh, swapped 'em around! Oh, I see!

1ST MAN: Yeah, I see.

2ND MAN: You've got to … oh that's easy to do.

1ST MAN: And there's 'North West nine point four' that should be 'South West'.

WOMAN: That's it, that's it.

2ND MAN: Right, OK. All right?

1ST MAN: Sorry about that.

WOMAN: OK, I've not finished yet. We've got some errors with the figures too. Now in the Wales figure, you've put 15.1 – are you with me? – but the original figure was 5.1, they've put an extra one in there, so correct that … that should be 5.1. And then the East Midlands on the right … now that is ridiculous. It says 69 per cent, that would be more than the South East, they've left out the decimal point, are you with me?

2ND MAN: 'cause the segment looks … it's way too small, innit?

WOMAN: Well it should be 6.9 per cent … put the decimal point in.

2ND MAN: What threw me with that was the East Midlands, I wasn't sure exactly what the area …

WOMAN: Yes, thank you, thank you, and the last one is just a small one, but I want to get it absolutely accurate. The figure for the South East is 35.0, not 34.0 … if you could correct that …

2ND MAN: It's one out, it's one out …

1ST MAN: It's one out. 35 …

2ND MAN: It all makes a difference, doesn't it?

WOMAN: So it reads 35.0, thank you …

2ND MAN: So, well, I mean, so that's it, then, is it?

WOMAN: Well, I think that's it, no, no, no, no, wait, you forgot the title. Now the title should read 'Share of the United Kingdom's …'

1ST / 2ND MAN: 'United Kingdom's'

WOMAN: Yeah, apostrophe Kingdom's number of businesses, and I want that at the top, please, is that clear?

1ST/2ND MAN: Number of businesses.

1ST MAN: 'Share of the United Kingdom's Number of Businesses.' Right, OK.

WOMAN: All right, now, moving on to the second chart …

1ST MAN: The bar-chart …

WOMAN: Yes, the bar-chart, the one which has nothing up the vertical axis, why? Well, the zero's there at the bottom, but you need to put 10, 20, 30, 40, etc. all the way up the vertical axis up to 60.

2ND MAN: Next to the little marks?

WOMAN: Yes, where those little marks are. Thank you. So – all the way up to 60.

1ST MAN: Well, I mean, that's not too bad, is it? If that's all that's wrong with it …

WOMAN: Apart from the fact that it makes the graph incomprehensible, no, not bad at all, but we've not finished yet, now, along the horizontal axis, if you look, you've only put the figures for the first three pairs of columns, so we've got 20-24, 25-30, 31-34 but then for some reason best known to yourselves, the rest are missing, why?

1ST MAN: I can't? honestly …

WOMAN: Could you please now put in 35-40, 41-44, 45-48 …

2ND MAN: They're going up in fives, aren't they, all the time?

WOMAN: 49-59, so we're increasing the band there and then the final one, please, sixty plus.

1ST MAN: Yes … what was the last one?

WOMAN: Sixty plus … that means more than sixty. Just do a little plus sign.

1ST MAN: I do know that.

WOMAN: Now and lastly, it says 'Hours' as the title for the horizontal axis, now what is that 'hours'? Per day, per week, per century, what? Be accurate, what is it?

1ST MAN: Well, I think it's … it's per week.

WOMAN: Well, write it in, then.

2ND MAN: Would be, wouldn't it? 'Hours … per week.'

1ST MAN: Right, is that it, d'you think?

WOMAN: Well, I think so, unless you can spot anything else.

1ST MAN: No, it looks fine, I'm very sorry about all these mistakes, it won't happen again.

WOMAN: There might not be an again.

Unit 15

15.9 Listening

PAUL: Lenny.

LENNY: This is from … a letter from Patrick Dixon who says that while at a friend's wedding in Birmingham last week I stayed at the Novis Hotel. The following is transcribed verbatim from the Welcome Pack in the hotel room. 'Non-smoking room. Non-smoking rooms are indicated by a non-smoking sign in the ashtray.'

PAUL: Harry.

HARRY: It's from Lewis's Shipping List. It says: Overdue vessel MV Astra Maris, Asuncion March 16th. Motor Vessel Astra Maris is overdue at Asuncion. She sailed from Buenos Aires on January 18th with a crew of twelve and 22,000 cases of whisky.

I just like the other one that I saw from the Canberra Morning Star, which says: 'Traditionally the bulk of Australia's imports have come from overseas.'

PAUL: Well before we start the gripping tie-breaker round, here's a story seen in the Daily Post.

RUTH: The anti-smoker international award went to Texas for banning convicts from having a last cigarette before the electric chair. (*Quiet laughter.*) Authorities said it was bad for their health.

PAUL: Alex?

ALEX: Yes, this clipping throws an interesting light on the privatisation of the railways. It's from the timetable of Linx South Central, which operates in the West Country and in the section entitled 'Other Information' there's this advice: 'Before leaving the train, please ensure that the station platform is there.'

PAUL: Yes, very cautious. Harry.

HARRY: Yes, I've got a cutting from the Chester Mail, Paul. Conducting his own defence, Mr Rupert Smee said that the house he lived in was a former brewery. 'Is it not possible,' he asked the court, 'that vibration from passing traffic could cause dust from old hops to fall into my tea, making it alcoholic?'

He was fined £200 and banned from driving for six months.

ANSWERS TO THE QUIZ ON PAGE 7:

1	a	4 points	b	3 points	c	0 points
2	a	2 points	b	0 points		
3	a	5 points	b	4 points	c	3 points
	d	2 points	e	0 points		
4	a	2 points	b	3 points	c	1 point
5	a	0 points	b	1 point	c	3 points
	d	1 point	e	2 points		
6	a	4 points	b	2 points	c	1 point
	d	0 points				
7	a	0 points	b	3 points	c	2 points
	d	1 point				
8	a	3 points	b	2 points	c	0 points
	d	0 points				
9	a	1 point	b	2 points	c	4 points
	d	1 point				
10	a	0 points	b	2 points	c	4 points
	d	2 points				

INTERPRETATION:

25–35: Congratulations! You fulfil most, if not all, of the conditions for learning a foreign language well. You understand the value of practice, of checking, and of meeting English speakers. You probably like the language, and are interested in language in general.

10–25: You are certainly well on the way to becoming a good language learner. It may be necessary for you to 'play to your strong points' – for example, you need to be realistic about your goals, and know exactly what you want, and the best way to get it. Don't forget that, even if you are not 'in love' with English, there are a lot of good habits which can help you in your studies.

1–9: Don't worry! You may be studying English for many different reasons, and every student varies in their approach to a foreign language. But keep in mind that, if you adopt some useful habits like always checking your work, practising as much as possible, and doing everything to revise new vocabulary, you can make loads of progress. And if you can find an English-speaking friend … so much the better!

ANSWERS TO THE GRAMMAR QUIZ ON PAGE 136: (MIXED UP)

a   No.

b   Because in the second case, the Minister has or owns the tie, and in this case you can only use the *'s* construction; in the first case, the Minister doesn't own the departure but simply departs, so either construction can be used.

c   Because in the first, the chicken has been killed and something is made from it, whereas in the second, it has produced something while still alive.

d   True. You can use the noun + noun construction to say where someone comes from.

e   *Treetop* is such a common expression that it has become a single word, but usually with expressions with *top, bottom, back, middle,* etc. (when they are <u>nouns not adjectives</u>) we use *of*.

f   The first is for dogs in general; the second is food that a particular dog is going to eat.

g   The first means the container with its contents; the second is only a specific kind of container.

h   Because we use *'s* with animals or people but not usually with inanimate objects.

i   Because *roadside* is a very common expression and so it has become a single word; *the side of the desk* is not so common and so the single word *deskside* has not developed.

j   Because in the first, the time is a general time; in the second it is a particular time.

k   False. Often you mean this but not always. In many cases the relationship between the two nouns is slightly different:

– *Peter's fax* would mean that Peter sent the fax; the first noun does something to the second.

– *a woman's dress* simply means that this kind of dress is used by a woman, not necessarily the possession of a particular woman; the first noun uses the second.

– *the Board's decision* would mean that the Board decided; the first noun does the second.

Thanks and acknowledgments

Our thanks go to students and staff at St. Clare's Oxford, Oxford English Centre, Atlas English, Oxford; Dr Graham Simpson; Mary Neal; Sue O'Connell. Thanks also to Roberta and Fiammetta for grinning (occasionally) and bearing it. We would also like to thank Annie Cornford and everybody at Cambridge University Press who has helped with this project, especially Niki Browne and Charlotte Adams. And finally, thanks to Justin Gosling for the ram-raid story in Unit 4.

The authors and publishers would like to thank the following teachers and advisors who trialled and commented on the material and whose feedback was invaluable.

Andrew Billingham, Slovakia; Lois Clegg, Italy; Wendy Gibbons, UK; Carmina Gregori, Spain; Maxine Harvey, Turkey; Charles Lambert, Italy; Régine Lambrech, France; Sean Murphy, Spain; Linda Ogden, Italy; Patricia O'Sullivan, UK; Simon Phipps, Turkey; Paul Sainsbury, Spain; Hatice Sofu, Turkey; Mauro R. Staiano, Czech Republic; Mereia Trenchs, Spain.

The authors and publishers are grateful to the following for permission to reproduce copyright material. It has not been possible to identify the sources of all the material used and in such cases the publishers would welcome information from copyright owners.

Graph on p. 9: *The Brain Book* by Peter Russel, Routledge; Text on p. 14: *Book of Childcare* by Hugh Jolly, with permission from Christopher Jolly; Text 2 on p. 15 and text on p. 22: *The Oxford Guide to Word Games* by Tony Augarde, Oxford University Press 1984, reproduced by permission of Oxford University Press; Text 3 on p. 15: *Wordpower* by Edward de Bono, Penguin; Article 1 on p. 25: 'The future for your body', © J. Sadgrove/*Marie-Claire*/IPC Magazines Ltd; Article 2 on p. 25: 'Work out wonder' by Nigel Hawkes, *The Times* 1995, ©Times Newspapers Limited 1995; Article 3 on p. 25: 'Eat, drink and be brainy' by Thoby Young, *The Sunday Telegraph* 1994, with permission of Thoby Young; Article 4 on p. 26: 'Off colour?', *Top Santé* 1994; Tips on p. 34: 'Ten tips from top travellers', © *Daily Mail*/Giles Milton 1995; 'Do I want to get away from it all? Give me a break ...' on p. 35: by Jean Moir, © *The Observer* 1996; 'The Origins of Policing' on p. 43: *The story of our police*. Crown copyright is reproduced with the permission of the Controller of Her Majesty's Stationery Office; Slogans on p. 44: National Neighbourhood Watch Association; Text on p. 52: by Liz Hunt, *The Independent* 1995; 'It hurts when you say Doctor, Mawhinney' on p. 60: by Ian Jack, *The Independent* 1996; Text on p. 61-62: The Real Meaning of Money by Dorothy Rowe, HarperCollins, reproduced by kind permission of the author and Lisa Eveleigh Literary Agency; Text on pp. 68-69: 'The NI interview with Marina Silva' by Tony Samphier, reproduced by permission of News-Scan International Limited; Text on p. 76: by Nick Craven, *The Daily Mirror*; Text on p. 81: *Made in America* by Bill Bryson, © Bill Bryson 1994, published by Black Swan, a division of Transworld Publishers Ltd. All rights reserved; Text on pp. 86-87: by Mary Budd Rowe, *Reader's Digest* 1996; Tables A to D on pp. 88-89: *Social Trends 27*, The Office for National Statistics, © Crown Copyright 1999; Article 1 on p. 94: by Stephen White, *The Daily Mirror*, 1997; Article 2 on p. 94: by David Ward, © *The Guardian* 1997; Text 1 on p. 97: 'Autistic boy survives swamps' by Charles Laurence, *The Daily Telegraph* 1996; Texts 2 and 5 on p. 97: *The Fortean Times* 1997; Text 3 on p. 97: *Neither Here Nor There* by Bill Bryson, © Bill Bryson 1991, published by Transworld Publishers Ltd. All rights reserved; Text 4 on p. 97: *The Evening Standard* 1996; Text 6 on p. 97: *The Daily Record* 1996; Text 1 on p. 104: 'In a family embrace' by Jan Morris, © *The Guardian* 1996; Text 3 on p. 105: *Barcelona* by Robert Hughes, The Harvill Press 1992, © Robert Hughes 1992. Reproduced by permission of the Harvill Press; Text 4 on p. 105: 'Valerie Singleton - Chelsea' by Guy Walters, *The Times* 1996, ©Times Newspapers Ltd 1996; Text 5 on p. 105: *The World Cities* by Peter Hall, Weidenfeld & Nicolson; Text 6 on p. 106: *Made in America* by Bill Bryson, © Bill Bryson 1994, published by Black Swan, a division of Transworld Publishers Ltd. Reproduced by permission of William Morrow and Company Inc. All rights reserved; List of entries on p. 109: *Practical English Language 2nd Edition* by Michael Swan, reproduced by permission of Oxford University Press, © Michael Swan 1980, 1995; 'Adjectives and adverbs' on p. 110: *Adanced Grammar in Use* by Martin Hewings, Cambridge University Press 1999; Text on p. 115: by Decca Aitkenhead, *The Independent* 1995; Text on p. 124: by Jonathan Sale, *The Independent* 1995, with permission from Jonathan Sale; Texts on pp. 133-134: 'Take two careers' by Rebecca Cripps, *Marie Claire*, © Rebecca Cripps/*Marie-Claire*/IPC Magazines; Bar graph on p. 139: *Social Trends 26*, The Office for National Statistics, © Crown Copyright 1997; Cartoons on p. 141: 'Arthur loves his new job at the fairground' by McLachlan, *Private Eye*; 'If you got a mobile phone ...' and 'Not at these prices...': *The Daily Mirror*; 'No dessert for you ...' and 'Whatever you do ...': *Close to home* by John McPherson, Andrews & McMeel; Text on p. 142: by Robert Matthews, *The Sunday Telegraph* 1994; Text on p. 145: *The Language of Humour* by Walter Nash, Addison Wesley Longman.

The authors and publishers are grateful to the following illustrators and photographic sources.

Illustrators:

Terry Hadler, Andrew Morris, Jacky Rough, David Thelwell, Kathryn Walker

Photographic sources:

(l) = left, (r) = right, (m) = middle, (t) = top, (b) = bottom

Bridgeman Art Library/Vatican Museums and Galleries for p. 121; Ciara Pike-Burke for p. 114 (m); Famous/Duval for p. 143; Gareth Boden/Cambridge University Press for pp. 129 (t) and 132 (r); Hulton Getty for p. 142 (b); Image Bank for pp. 42 (mr), 98, 132 (l); PA Photos/Sean Dempsey for p. 77; Pictor International for pp. 21 (r), 33 (r), 42 (tr), 59 (m), 59 (b), 111, 123 (r), 123 (l); Rex Features for pp. 24 (t), 34, 42 (tl), 42 (b), 42 (lm), 59 (t), 137, 141, 142 (t); Stock Market/Jose Fuste Raga for p. 114 (b); Superstock for pp. 85 (b), 114, The Lowe Museum, The University of Miami 114 (br), /Musee du Louvre, Paris 114 (tm); The National Lottery for p. 60; Tony Stone Images for pp. /D Young Wolff 9, /Don Smetzer 14, /Steven Peters 21 (l), /Christopher Bissel 21 (t), /Lori Adamski Peek 24 (b), /Lorne Resnick 24 (m), /Donna Day 24 (r) and 51 (r), /Tom Bean 33 (b), /Richard Passmore 33 (l), /Nick Dolding 51 (l), /Steve Outram 52, /Simon Battensby 59 (l), /Renee Lynn 67 (b), /Paul Edmondson 67 (rm) and 69, /John Warden 67 (l), /Nicholas Parfitt 67 (tr), /David Endersbee 79, /Arthur Tilley 85 (l), /Andy Sacks 85 (r), /Peter Pearson 103 (b), /Claire Hayden 103 (r), /Shaun Egan 103 (l), /Lineka 112, /Andrea Booher 129 (b).

Freelance picture research by Rebecca Watson.

Book and cover by Pentacor plc, High Wycombe

The cassette which accompanies this book was produced by James Richardson at Studio AVP, London.